PRAISE FOR WILLIAM CANE'S

The Art of Kissing

"Get it and expand your puckering portfolio." —*Seventeen*

"You are bound to learn something new about kissing if you read this book." —*Newton Bee* (Newton, Connecticut)

"*The Art of Kissing* goes beyond the valley of French kissing by exploring . . . such advanced exercises as the underwater kiss, the counterkiss, and the electric kiss (rub your stockinged feet on the carpet and *whoa!*)." —*Washington Times*

"Whoever said 'a kiss is just a kiss' didn't get his mitts on *The Art of Kissing* . . . a detailed how-to book . . . this year's handy alternative to chocolates." —*Elle*

"It's refreshing to think about kissing per se rather than as a prelude to something else." —*Self*

"If you . . . want to smooch like Rick and Ilsa in *Casablanca,* this bussing bible is for you." —*Lowell Sun* (Massachusetts)

"Some terrific tips on how you can make every kiss as passionate and thrilling as your first."   —*The National Enquirer*

"I advise you to race full speed to your bookstore and pick up a copy of *The Art of Kissing* . . . it could save you emotional problems."
                                        —*Clarion Ledger* (Jackson, Mississippi)

"*The Art of Kissing* is perhaps the most thorough encyclopedia on swapping slobber ever available. . . . Cane covers every kind of kissing imaginable. . . . Whether you're looking to improve your skills or to save your hide after giving a lousy Valentine's Day gift, *The Art of Kissing* is sure to be effective."
                                                —*Richardson News* (Texas)

"The definitive book . . . lighthearted . . . fun . . . worth more than lip service!"   —*Oxford Mail* (England)

Also by William Cane

THE ART OF KISSING

THE BOOK OF KISSES

THE ART OF HUGGING

THE ART OF KISSING
BOOK OF QUESTIONS
AND ANSWERS

St. Martin's Griffin
New York

Kiss
Like a
Star

SMOOCHING SECRETS
from the
SILVER SCREEN

William Cane

www.stmartins.com

Book design by Jennifer Ann Daddio

Library of Congress Cataloging-in-Publication Data

Cane, William.
    Kiss like a star : smooching secrets from the silver screen / William Cane.
        p. cm.
    Includes index.
    ISBN-13: 978-0-312-35993-5
    ISBN-10: 0-312-35993-4
    1. Kissing. 2. Kissing—Pictorial works. 3. Kissing in motion pictures. 4. Kissing in motion pictures—Pictorial works. I. Title.

GT2640.C364 2007
394—dc22

2006051159

First Edition: February 2007

1   3   5   7   9   10   8   6   4   2

To Lester Packer,
for his research into antioxidants

And to you, dear reader,
for your
unflagging interest in kissing

Contents

Part Two—The French Kiss and Other Advanced Kisses

Part Three—Kissing Techniques

Acknowledgments

I'm indebted to Ray Carney of Boston University for his suggestions and insights into film criticism. Naturally I take full responsibility for the opinions expressed in the following pages and for any inadvertent errors or omissions. Thanks to friends and family for their support and help as I did the research for this book. I'm grateful also to the staff at Kim's Mediatronics for their suggestions on film kisses; to my attorneys, Mark L. Beigelman and Gary M. Emmanuel, for their counsel; to my literary agent, Carla Glasser, for her advice; to my lecture agents, Kevin and Jayne Moore, at the Contemporary Issues Agency; and to Marilyn, my wife, for her encouragement and assistance.

Last but not least, I'd like to dedicate this book to you, dear reader. Your purchase of this volume goes a long way toward helping me to continue doing research into kissing.

Introduction

You are about to enter a new world simply by opening this book, a world where *you* are the star and can kiss with the flair, passion, and romantic intensity of the most recognizable Hollywood actors.

I've selected scenes from modern and classic films to inspire you to try something new. From each film you'll discover useful approaches to kissing, and from each actor you'll pick up pointers on technique. By the end of the book you'll be familiar with some of the most romantic, thrilling, and exciting kisses. This in itself should add magic to your kissing experiences. Every kiss is described in detail, and the accompanying photos will show you how to do each one. For best results, especially when doing something like the vacuum kiss or the French kiss, you'll want to watch the film and actually *see* that kiss in action.

To date I've surveyed more than one hundred thousand people across the United States and in twenty-three other countries on every aspect of kissing, so I know a lot about the people who read my books. I know you wish you could experience romantic, passionate, thrilling kisses—the kind you've seen in *Gone With the Wind, Titanic,* and *When Harry Met Sally.* This book will respond to that desire and usher you into a new world of kissing enjoyment. We'll begin our journey with the most romantic kisses on film. Then we'll explore the French kiss and other advanced kisses. Finally, we'll visit the most sophisticated and essential kissing techniques—all things you've seen in the movies and dreamed *you* could try yourself. I promise you that by the time you finish the journey, your kissing will not only be modern, contemporary, and up-to-date, but timeless, creative, and above all romantic.

PART ONE

Romantic Kisses

Movie kisses can seem especially romantic because of background music, setting, and storyline. But your kisses can be even more romantic, and you don't need any of those frills. All you need is contained in the chapters that follow. The first step is to realize that your emotions are the key to romantic kisses. The second step is to use some of the ideas in the following pages when you're with the one you love. Rest assured that a properly executed surprise kiss, neck kiss, or goodbye kiss will foster intimacy and bring out the best in you and your partner. If you also happen to be in a nice setting and have some music on in the background, that certainly won't hurt.

Romantic Kissing

THREE THINGS are essential for a romantic kiss: a loving relationship, a powerful emotion, and Humphrey Bogart. The kiss between Rick and Ilsa (Ingrid Bergman) in *Casablanca* (1942) has all the elements of a great romantic kiss.

The kiss begins inauspiciously with Ilsa pointing a gun at Rick and demanding that he hand over certain important documents. I don't recommend beginning a kiss like this, but the fact is that these two people love each other, only they don't know it yet. Rick mistakenly thinks that Ilsa is only after the documents and that she cares nothing for him. Ilsa mistakenly thinks that he doesn't really care for her and is selfish. When he dares her to shoot him, a powerful emotion overcomes Ilsa and a tear falls from her eye as she recalls her love for Rick. As a prelude to a romantic kiss, arousing almost any strong emotion will suffice, but feelings of regret, of lost opportunity, and of longing are probably at the top of the list. There are, of course, easier ways to arouse powerful emotions than by straining your relationship to the breaking point, as is done here, and in many cases all you need to do is whisper a few sweet words of endearment to your partner to get a romantic reaction and set the stage for the kiss.

Before long Rick and Ilsa have a moment of realization: They now know that they love each other, that despite the obstacles between them—including the fact that Ilsa is married to another man—there's still a strong current linking them to their past affair in Paris, and that if nothing else, they have their love to fall back on in this time of stress (the film is set during World War II). At this point they draw closer and their lips are only inches apart.

As you move into a romantic kiss, it often helps to pause and slow things down to a glacial pace as Rick and Ilsa do. That will build romantic tension and make the ensuing kiss more tender and sweet.

Bogart and Bergman are at the top of their form in this scene, moving together slowly and gently for a memorable film kiss. *Casablanca,* of course, is the movie in which the words "a kiss is just a kiss" are sung, but this scene proves those words ironic, since their kiss is actually quite deep with meaning and powerful emotion. May all your romantic kisses be as sweet.

Romantic Kissing

AT GUNPOINT Ilsa points a gun at Rick, but he doesn't flinch. He's so in love with her he doesn't care if he dies. The first fundamental for a romantic kiss is in place—the man loves the woman.

A TEAR Remembering how much she loved him in Paris, Ilsa sheds a tear, giving us the second fundamental for a good romantic kiss—the woman loves the man.

MOVING IN The third fundamental—a romantic setting—is also in place. They're alone, they're close, they're looking into each other's eyes.

BOGART AND BERGMAN Humphrey Bogart moves in slowly and kisses with passion and a sensitive touch. Tender kisses like these are like wordless questions to the recipient. Ingrid Bergman almost melts into his arms for the perfect romantic reply.

Gentle Kissing

GENTLE KISSING lets you take your time, and when done in a romantic setting, as it is in the film *A Beautiful Mind* (2001), it can signal the turning point of a relationship, allowing two people to discover how much they really care for each other. The scene opens near a lake where John (Russell Crowe) and Alicia (Jennifer Connelly) are having a picnic, and before long their innocent conversation leads to a growing intimacy. Alicia leans forward and lowers her eyes, preparing for a gentle kiss, and John does the same, mirroring her actions with a leisurely response to her movements. At this point their noses have already passed, both having tilted their heads ever so slightly, and as they close the final few inches they slow down so that their lip contact will be feather soft and lovingly sweet.

They're essentially just gently touching lips, hardly even opening their mouths, instead letting their lips do all the work. Sometimes tender kisses like this are the best way to communicate romantic feelings. Notice that John, with his eyes closed, simply lets his lower lip rest on Alicia's as he moves his head slowly back and forth.

As the kiss progresses John becomes even more receptive, still with eyes closed, contentedly letting Alicia brush her lower lip against his upper lip. He has, in effect, let her take control of the kiss. To relinquish control to your partner now and then allows her to come up with her own creative ideas. It also ensures that the kiss will remain leisurely and gentle, especially if your partner is of like mind, as Alicia is here. Notice that she has her eyes closed too, concentrating on the feel of the kiss and enjoying the softness of John's light technique. By the time the kiss has gone on for a few seconds they both seem to have been hypnotized by the pleasant experience of their gentle lip contact. You can get the same otherworldly effect by using a light touch and a restrained, gentle kissing approach.

Gentle Kissing

BUILDING ROMANCE Nothing builds romance like gazing sweetly into your partner's eyes during a pleasant conversation. The setting is also important for romance to blossom: Here, John and Alicia enjoy a lakeside panorama, but they seem to be focusing on each other.

MIRRORING ACTIONS Gentle kissing is impossible unless both kissers are moving slowly and softly. By mirroring Alicia's slowness and gentleness, John ensures that the kiss will be a tender experience.

FEATHER-LIGHT KISSING Gentle kissing is easy to do—all it takes is a certain presence of mind and a willingness to relax and let your lips follow your partner's lead, as John is doing here.

RELINQUISHING CONTROL Here John has relinquished control of the kiss to Alicia. Notice that his mouth is open, but he's not rushing into a French kiss or putting pressure on her; instead, he's letting Alicia set the direction and pace as she brushes her lower lip gently against his upper lip.

The
Surprise Kiss

MOST PEOPLE LIKE being surprised with a kiss. It's exciting, stimulating, and often leaves the recipient glowing with pleasure. A memorable example of the surprise kiss appears at the end of *An Officer and a Gentleman* (1982) when Zack (Richard Gere) sneaks up on Paula (Debra Winger) at her job.

The surprise occurs while Paula is working in a factory. Zack enters, dressed in his white military uniform and looking handsome and dashing, but Paula—who is wearing earplugs to protect herself from the loud machinery—neither hears nor sees him. Taking advantage of the fact that Paula is so engrossed in her work that she hasn't noticed him, Zack walks up behind her and stands for a moment, apparently trying to decide what to do. Then he leans down and quickly kisses the back of her neck. The kiss is such a surprise to Paula that she hardly knows how to react. She looks startled and amazed. This element of shock is what makes a surprise kiss so memorable since it really gets the adrenaline going. And a surprise kiss in public packs a double wallop of excitement because the recipient is being *seen* while she's being surprised.

Zack's surprise kiss is not the end of their interaction—it's only the beginning. Paula turns around and kisses Zack, and things get more romantic after that. Zack picks her up and hugs her to his chest in a move of endearment not often seen outside the movies. As the scene continues he carries Paula through the factory, parading her past cheering and applauding co-workers as they exit together.

A surprise kiss like the one in *An Officer and a Gentleman* is a perfect way to say hello after a separation, and your partner doesn't even have to be wearing earplugs for you to achieve this element of surprise. All you need is the lucky chance to happen upon her when she's unaware of your presence. A quick kiss on the shoulder, the back of the neck, or anyplace that will tickle her fancy can leave a lasting impression and put a smile on her face. That's the special reward of the surprise kiss.

The Surprise Kiss

THE OPPORTUNITY TO SURPRISE A surprise kiss is often an impulsive action born of opportunity and romantic imagination. Here, Zack has a perfect opportunity because Paula has not heard or seen him enter.

A SURPRISE KISS This kiss can startle your partner, so it's a good idea to make sure she's not going to be too frightened. Zack sees that although Paula is working on a machine, she's safe enough to kiss.

REASSURING Because a surprise kiss can make pulses pound and hearts race, it's nice to have a reassuring kiss afterward. Zack and Paula enjoy a moment of affection after their surprise kiss. This reassurance is especially helpful for the recipient of the kiss, who may still be somewhat shocked.

GETTING CARRIED AWAY WITH KISSING The movie ends with Zack carrying Paula out of the factory, kissing as they go. A surprise kiss doesn't always have such an exciting sequel, but it always leaves an impression no other kiss can match.

Kissing the Face

BECAUSE LIPS HAVE such strong sensual connotations, an expression of tenderness and all-encompassing love can sometimes get lost in a lip kiss. At times of great emotional crisis it's often more appropriate to kiss the entire face rather than simply the lips. A memorable example appears at the emotional conclusion to Jane Campion's *The Piano* (1993). Ada (Holly Hunter) is a mute from Scotland who falls in love with George (Harvey Keitel) in New Zealand. At the end of the film they're reunited. George is so happy to have her back that he doesn't simply kiss her lips, he kisses her entire face. This action deserves comment because it represents a special emotional meeting between two people—the one who gives the kiss and the one who understands enough to receive it properly.

The kiss commences when George kisses Ada's mouth, a natural enough place from which to launch a series of kisses since the mouth is the spot we usually kiss. But George's emotions are so overwhelming that a lip kiss can't satisfy him. He moves to

Ada's nose for a quick peck and then up to her eyes, which Ada closes to receive his straying tender kisses. The eyes are a romantic spot, of course, but the combination of lips, nose, eyes, and cheek make this more than a simple romantic kiss; in fact, it becomes an especially moving expression of all-consuming love. The culmination of the kiss occurs when George kisses Ada's neck, holding her arms tightly as if he can't bear the thought of ever letting her go. A neck kiss like this—quick on the heels of other face kisses—suggests, again, an all-encompassing love, one that will keep two people together with bonds of friendship and understanding. When the situation is emotional, especially at a reunion or reconciliation, and when you want to express your all-embracing love, move beyond the lips and kiss the entire face. You'll be saying something very special that will be heard loud and clear.

Kissing the Face

THE LIPS George kisses the lips but this is just the first step. When your feelings are overwhelming, lip kisses may not be enough.

THE NOSE Moving upward, he even kisses her nose. Ada doesn't complain. She seems to understand that he needs all of her, and that he's expressing his deep love with this wandering kiss.

THE EYES He moves his hands to caress her face as he gently kisses her eyes.

THE NECK The neck, too, receives attention in a complete face kiss. Afterward it is appropriate to return to the lips. Kissing the face like this says more than words about how completely you love someone.

The Cradle Kiss

A SENTIMENTAL KISS that exists in a class all by itself, the cradle kiss works on many levels, conjuring up ideas of shelter and protection. For this reason it's a kiss that no serious lover should neglect. When you want to express your love at its tenderest, most vulnerable, and most wonderful, the cradle kiss will work its magic every time. Perhaps the most memorable example of the kiss appears in *Bus Stop* (1956).

The kiss begins with Bo (Don Murray), a naïve cowboy from Montana, talking in a cozy bus stop diner with Cherie (Marilyn Monroe), the girl he loves. He's been pursuing her in his crazy way, kidnapping her and taking her on a wild bus trip through the snow. She confesses that she's not the kind of girl he thought she was, she did more than sing in the saloon where he met her. Her checkered past doesn't bother Bo, and his persevering love makes Cherie fall for her abductor despite his lumbering ways. At this point, Bo sets the kiss in motion by raising his hands above her neck. The second phase of the kiss continues smoothly from the first, with Bo raising his hands even higher, cupping Cherie's face. The cradle kiss really can't work if your partner isn't a willing participant. In this scene Cherie is certainly a willing participant: she looks directly into Bo's eyes as he positions his hands, demonstrating that she trusts him and that she cares for him.

In the third phase of the kiss, Bo looks troubled for a moment. This is a key point in the kiss because it gives him time to say something sweet. "When you kiss somebody for serious," he says, "it's kind of scary." The line is delivered with so much feeling that it seems to electrify Cherie. She has finally found a man who loves and respects her despite her past. The technique to be remembered is that right in the middle of the cradle kiss, when your hands are around your lover's face, you can pause, like Bo, and utter some sweet words that will thrill and charm your partner.

The fourth phase of the kiss is the reply phase. Just before being kissed, Cherie says, "Yes, it is." It's nice to say something loving at this moment, but silence is also an option. What is not optional, however, is the eye contact, which you must maintain as you segue into the kiss itself. Notice how Cherie gazes back lovingly at Bo. The last phase of the cradle kiss is actual lip contact. Bo leans forward and gently kisses Cherie, keeping his hands around her face all the time. In the final analysis, the cradle kiss is a wonderfully romantic gesture that will help you express tender feelings no matter where you are.

The Cradle Kiss

CRADLING Bo begins the physical setup by raising his hands. He relies on Cherie to accept his caress. The cradle kiss suggests tenderness, so it is usually accepted as a romantic gesture. Notice that Cherie looks comfortable and ready to be kissed.

CHARMING Bo charms Cherie by saying something nice just before the kiss. More important than the exact words is the tone of voice used. Bo is all choked up with emotion, and his voice communicates deep feelings.

COMFORTING Cherie comforts Bo by replying sweetly. A reply is optional, but eye contact is a necessity. Looking directly back at him, Cherie parts her lips to signal that she's ready to be kissed.

CONSUMMATING Leaning forward, Bo consummates the cradle kiss, carefully keeping his hands around Cherie's face. When cradle kissing, you can keep your hands in this loving position until you finish the lip-contact phase, ensuring a loving embrace throughout.

The Impetuous Kiss

LOVE IS MADNESS. Indeed, without madness love wouldn't be so grand. Sometimes it's sweet, sometimes it's tender, but often—in even the best of circumstances—it's madly impetuous. The very nature of love demands, therefore, that a lover know how to give, and receive, an impetuous kiss. Hollywood loves such kisses because they're often turning points in a story. You too can experience the thrill of an impetuous kiss and go through your very own personal transformations by following the techniques used by Macaulay "Mike" Connor (James Stewart) and Tracy Lord (Katharine Hepburn) in *The Philadelphia Story* (1940).

The scene opens with Mike talking with Tracy in the garden. They're having a little argument. For lovers, this is par for the course. No relationship on earth is without its small discords now and then. But there are ways out of them, and this particular scene shows you how to turn a conflict into a kiss. After their heated discussion, Tracy storms away from Mike in a huff and leaves him stranded and alone. What lover hasn't felt abandoned once in a while? But this discord gives Mike an opportunity to patch things up, *if* he can only figure out how to approach Tracy.

After a moment's hesitation, he strides over to Tracy, who stands with her back to him. Instead of confronting your sweetheart face-to-face, try Mike Connor's approach and confront her at right angles. It's much less threatening and ultimately will work much better for you, just as it does for Mike.

Next he pivots Tracy around to face him, turning her quickly like a ballerina. And Tracy, for her part, helps out with this crucial move by pivoting toward him. No woman can be turned around so easily unless she secretly wishes to have a reconciliation—or a kiss. Hopefully your partner will be as willing as Tracy proves to be in this scene.

Mike is uncertain about testing the waters with a kiss, but he goes for it anyway. With passion and force, he pulls Tracy to his chest and mashes his lips against hers. When you kiss like this you get a chance to see how your partner will react to your impetuous behavior. If you don't get slapped, you may just get lucky and receive a kiss in return. Mike makes all the right moves, and Tracy gives as good as she gets, looking up into his eyes and kissing him back with feeling.

Once you've gone through such a harrowing experience, a sort of turning point in a relationship, you may need a few seconds to simmer down and confirm the good thing that has just happened. Almost bewildered by the experience, Tracy and Mike stand together embracing for a while, as if to acknowledge that they have, indeed, come through a rough patch together. Using these same tactics, you can turn your impetuous feelings into kisses that bring the two of you closer together. And isn't that, after all, what romantic kissing is all about?

The Impetuous Kiss

ARGUING Mike and Tracy are having an argument, and it's so heated that Tracy is getting set to walk away from him. The question is: Can Mike turn the situation around with an impetuous kiss?

CONFRONTING Following quickly, Mike confronts Tracy. But he doesn't stand face-to-face with her, which might be considered too threatening. Instead he approaches from a right angle and seizes her upper arms. Try the same angular approach next time you want a reconciliation.

PIVOTING With a quick motion, Mike pivots Tracy around to face him. If a girl doesn't want to be reconciled with you, she won't let herself be turned so easily. Tracy, however, almost spins on her own, she's so eager for a make-up kiss.

TESTING Still uncertain of her feelings, Mike tests the waters with an impetuous kiss. Tracy loves the kiss and kisses him back. Your results may vary, but one thing is certain—you've got to try an impetuous kiss if you expect to turn a bad situation around.

The Talking Kiss

TALKING WHILE KISSING is not only possible, it's virtually mandatory if you consider yourself a good lover. Some girls like to be told jokes while French kissing. Some boys like to pay compliments to their partner. The point is, you don't have to recite the Constitution, all you need to do is learn the fine art of the talking kiss. A wonderful example of this kiss appears in Gus Van Sant's *To Die For* (1995).

A talking kiss usually occurs in the context of an ongoing conversation. Our scene begins with Jimmy Emmett (Joaquin Phoenix) lying on a bed talking with Suzanne Stone Maretto (Nicole Kidman). Before any talking kiss, it often helps if you establish a topic so that you can continue in the same vein once the kissing begins. While they're talking, Suzanne is simultaneously seducing Jimmy. She leans down over him on the bed, her face only a foot and a half from his, and she urges him to do what she wants. She appears to be in control, concentrating on the conversation, looking Jimmy directly in the eyes. This is a good way to act at the outset of a talking kiss. Eye contact and talking will develop a deep rapport which will intensify in the next part of the kiss.

To add urgency to what she's telling him, Suzanne leans down until her lips are directly over Jimmy's, their mouths only inches apart. From this close you can feel the heat from your partner's face on yours. You can use the same technique, leaning close to talk with your partner and getting your mouths within only one or two inches of each other's. This proximity almost always ensures that your conversation—no matter what you're talking about—will take on added romantic overtones. In fact, at this point you *could* talk about the Constitution and it would be romantic simply because you're so close.

Suzanne pauses occasionally while talking, with her lips hanging right over Jimmy's. This slight delay builds erotic tension. You can use the same approach, pausing with your lips poised close to your partner's. Your goal is to make him a little confused so that he doesn't know whether he wants to talk or to kiss.

When the moment is right Suzanne gives Jimmy a kiss, but all the time she's still continuing their conversation. When you kiss and talk right into your partner's mouth you connect on an intellectual level through your words and on an emotional level through the closeness of your faces and the contact of your lips. Hopefully this scene will inspire you to try some talking kisses. Just remember to keep the conversation light.

The Talking Kiss

CONVERSATION The context of a conversation is a great way to start a talking kiss. Jimmy talks to Suzanne from bed.

CONCENTRATION Suzanne concentrates on their conversation. You can use the same technique, continuing to talk as you move closer to seduce your lover.

HESITATION Suzanne kisses Jimmy and then hesitates midkiss, talking right into his mouth.

COMMUNICATION The talking kiss is a fun way to break up the routine of a regular kiss. The element of communication in a talking kiss is much less important than the romantic connection it fosters. Every relationship could use a little communication like this.

The Eye Kiss

AN EYE KISS is one of the most romantic kisses, perhaps because you have to be extra careful and delicate with your technique. A good example of this kiss appears in Edward Burns's *She's the One* (1996). Francis (Mike McGlone) has just proposed to Heather (Cameron Diaz). Of course he has no idea that an eye kiss is coming, so his eyes are open and he's smiling broadly. You may be surprised when someone leans in to kiss you on or near the eyes since it's an unusual spot for a kiss.

Heather is tickled by his proposal, but she doesn't know whether she wants to accept it. She needs time to think about it, so her reply will not be a kiss on the lips, which might signal acceptance, but instead the more distant, yet nonetheless romantic, eye kiss. Make your kissing choices wisely and you'll be on your way to kissing success since it's often the *kind* of kiss you give that makes the biggest impression.

When you decide to give an eye kiss, it helps to look at or near the eye that you intend to kiss. This can subtly alert the recipient as to where you'll kiss him. When Heather actually leans forward to kiss Francis's eye, she puts both hands on him to steady herself. Her right hand is around his neck, her left gently under his chin. Use a similarly careful caress so that your lips connect with the exact spot and at just the right time. Of course an eye kiss shouldn't be done on *open* eyes; as you lean forward, your partner should close his eyes so that you can gently touch your lips there. Heather kisses lightly over Francis's left eye, just a quick soft peck that says romance loud and clear. Francis, as predicted, has closed his eyes to receive the kiss.

When someone leans in to give you an eye kiss, make it easy and close your eyes momentarily. When the kiss is over and the lips have left your face, open your eyes and give your partner a smile, or better yet, an eye kiss in return.

The Eye Kiss

EYE CONTACT Francis proposes. Not knowing an eye kiss is in the works, his eyes are wide open, looking at Heather.

PROCRASTINATING Heather procrastinates. She needs time to think it over, so she decides to give him an eye kiss instead of a lip kiss. When you need some psychological distance but still want to be sweet and romantic, the eye kiss is the one to use.

PREPARING FOR THE KISS Heather prepares herself by gently holding Francis's neck and jaw. Steadying yourself for an eye kiss is a good idea.

PERFORMING THE EYE KISS The performance of an eye kiss requires timing, tact, and technique. You don't want to do it too fast, you want the occasion to be right, and you want to be gentle.

The Make-up Kiss

ONE OF THE BEST make-up kisses in film history occurs in *A Streetcar Named Desire* (1951). The kiss is preceded by a fight between Stanley (Marlon Brando) and his wife, Stella (Kim Hunter). Although the two love each other, they don't see eye to eye about Stella's sister coming to live with them.

As the scene begins, Stanley has been acting brutish, drinking and playing cards with his buddies. Suddenly a fight erupts between Stanley, Stella's sister, and Stanley's friends. During the brawl, Stella rips Stanley's T-shirt and then runs upstairs with her baby to stay with neighbors. Stanley pleads with her to come down with the famous cry: "Stella!"

After a few moments Stella comes downstairs slowly, as if drawn to him by animal magnetism, and the closer she gets the more the scene heats up. Every reconciliation kiss will be different, of course, but in every case one of the parties must approach the other. Stella approaches Stanley, and in a show of her true feelings she clutches him to her and puts her hands behind his head, her fingers entwined in his hair. They begin to embrace immediately. At this stage of a make-up kiss, when you have summoned up the courage to reach out to your partner, there is always the possibility of rejection. In fact, this is the most crucial stage of a make-up kiss, and the action in this classic scene is quite protracted, with Stella pressing her fingers into Stanley's back as he holds her, signaling that they're together again and that she loves him. The turning point in any argument is the moment when this love and desire is communicated with a touch, an embrace, or a kiss.

In preparation for the make-up kiss itself, Stella wraps her arms around Stanley, and he picks her up. Now both are at their emotional breaking point, and both are ready to mend the problems between them. They're ready for the kiss. There comes a time in any reconciliation when you know that things are going to work out at last, and that moment occurs here when Stella kisses Stanley on the lips as he carries her back into their New Orleans apartment. The actual make-up kiss itself—that is, the lip contact—is really only fleeting, but it is that contact that's the important moment in any reconciliation. Once it has occurred, things can start getting back to normal.

The problems between Stanley and Stella aren't *completely* eradicated by their make-up kiss, but they certainly have moved their relationship to a new level, and after that things will begin to improve.

The Make-up Kiss

"STELLA!" Stanley wants to patch things up with his wife. When he calls her name, he cries out his need for reconciliation. Brando's sheer animal magnetism is especially evident in this scene.

RECONCILIATION To the surprise of neighbors, Stella goes to Stanley almost like an automaton, drawn by his physical presence and his loving cry. It takes two to make a reconciliation, and these two are obviously on the same wavelength as Stella caresses Stanley's head.

TAKING A RISK In every make-up kiss there is an element of risk since you may be rejected as you try to reconcile your differences. Stanley takes a risk in calling out to Stella, and she takes a risk in going to him.

MAKING UP All good make-up kisses will be emotional experiences and will bridge any gap that has opened between two lovers.

The Neck Kiss

ONE OF THE MOST important kisses for a man to understand is the neck kiss because of all the places women like to be kissed, their favorite spot, aside from the mouth, happens to be the neck. The film *Breaking Up* (1997) contains a magnificent example of the neck kiss in action. Steve (Russell Crowe) and Monica (Salma Hayek) are dancing at night at poolside and Steve gets the idea to lean his partner back for a Hollywood kiss (see page 96). As he leans her back he suddenly finds that he has access to her neck. For one long moment he's looking at her neck and his lips are poised over it. The first thing to keep in mind when giving a neck kiss is that from a certain angle a woman's neck will be easier to reach and kiss, especially when she's leaning back. Because more of the neck is exposed, the kiss is easier to do. In most other positions you may have to brush her hair aside to get access to her neck, although even this move can tickle her fancy because simply touching and brushing her hair can be stimulating.

Before giving a neck kiss it's usually a good idea to begin on the lips; this will prepare your partner for the neck kiss itself. As he leans down toward Monica's neck, Steve has already prepared her by the romantic position of their bodies. When you lean your partner back in a dramatic fashion like Steve has done, it's almost always understood that you'll kiss her momentarily, and this is precisely what he does. One of the key techniques Steve uses is to move from one side of the neck to the other. This is a highly recommended procedure since for most women the entire neck is very sensitive. Another strategy he employs is to let his lips occasionally return to her mouth, then move back to the neck again. Including some lip kisses while kissing the neck will keep a woman satisfied since each body part transmits its own impulses to the brain.

For many men, discovering the power of the neck kiss will have special rewards since they'll see their partner thoroughly enjoy this relatively easy kiss. Once you discover the joys of the neck kiss, you owe it to yourself to try the special variation used in *Breaking Up*. If you lean her back and kiss her neck, she'll almost certainly get weak in the knees.

The Neck Kiss

DANCING IN THE DARK A neck kiss can start in any number of ways, but dancing is a wonderful preparation because it warms your partner up and gets her moving—perfect preludes to a neck kiss.

LEANING HER BACK Leaning Monica back for a dramatic Hollywood kiss, Steve sets the stage for the neck kiss. Notice that from this angle Monica's hair falls straight back and out of the way, so Steve doesn't even have to brush it aside.

KISSING HER NECK With a tender and feathery light touch, Steve moves his lips down until they just barely touch Monica's neck. Because the neck affords such a large area to be kissed, there's plenty of potential for moving along its length, including up to the ears and around to the nape of the neck.

FROM SIDE TO SIDE Steve uses the technique of kissing from side to side on Monica's neck. Notice that Monica seems to have gone into a trance, she's enjoying it so much.

Reunion Kisses

REUNIONS CAN BE extremely heartwarming and the kisses shared during these special moments can do much to bring two lovers back together by reuniting their lips as well as their hearts. A beautiful example of a reunion kiss occurs in *Cold Mountain* (2003).

Set at the time of the Civil War, this kiss between Ada (Nicole Kidman) and Inman (Jude Law) takes place in a fire-lit cabin on a snowy evening. It begins with a few words exchanged face to face and eye to eye. Sometimes reunions don't allow even this kind of rudimentary greeting because people rush right ahead into the kiss, but here the words Ada and Inman exchange are very romantic, and it's absolutely appropriate to say something sweet and loving before such a reunion kiss. In the next moment they're kissing, and the feeling in their hearts is expressed in their tender exchange: he's soft and sweet in his initial kisses, and she's gentle and receptive but also welcoming and warm. No two lovers can kiss like this without feeling something deep within them, something that brings them back to the place where they were before their separation. Their reunion kiss goes a long way toward bringing them back into that loving embrace they missed during Inman's absence. He was a soldier, she was a woman waiting for his return, now they're together again and their reunion kisses reflect their love better than words alone could ever do.

But a reunion kiss is also a time of stress, just as a goodbye kiss is a time of stress. And in times of stress human contact like that between Ada and Inman is soothing and restoring. Ada's feelings and the stress she feels are mirrored in her smile, a smile that one can often see breaking out on the lips of lovers in moments of passionate and intense kissing. She smiles and loves at the same time, and Inman apparently knows that this is not a mocking rebuke but instead a smile that lets her express relief at seeing him again.

After she smiles they kiss once more, and their welcoming embrace becomes a passionate kiss where she closes her eyes and lets her lips brush slowly and sensually against his. Both experienced kissers, they also take a moment now and then to break off from the kiss to enjoy each other's loving smile. This kind of reunion does more than bring things back to the way they were before he left. Like any good reunion kiss, it unites and also looks forward to the joy of being together again, to the pleasure of not having to long for each other, and to the comfort of knowing that he's home to stay.

Reunion Kisses

WORDS OF WELCOME Ada and Inman may exchange words of welcome but that's hardly sufficient to contain their feelings. They're overwhelmed by the fact that they're together again. A reunion kiss is needed at this moment.

WELCOMING KISSES Tender and sweet, their reunion kiss is more than a welcome: it also expresses all their relief and joy at being reunited.

SMILES OF JOY Ada's smile is a welcome sight to Inman. Reunions are momentous occasions, and kissing, smiling, and embracing are the best way to show you care.

PROMISES WITHOUT WORDS The reunion kiss can become passionate, especially if the two are young lovers, like Ada and Inman; but more than passion is communicated here. A reunion kiss may also be a promise to love more completely in the future than one has loved in the past.

The
Cheek Kiss

POSSIBLY THE MOST underrated of kisses, the cheek kiss may at first appear tame when compared to lip kisses or French kisses, but the cheek kiss has its own special charm, and it can express tenderness and romantic love better than most other lip contact. The cheek kiss can also serve as the launching point for more intimate kisses, and an exceptional example of the kiss, illustrating exactly how it can lead to other kisses, appears in *Raging Bull* (1980) in the scene where boxer Jake La Motta (Robert De Niro) kisses Vickie (Cathy Moriarty).

The kiss begins with Jake kissing Vickie for the first time—on the cheek. He is rather deliberate about this initial contact, taking his time and working up to it slowly, approaching Vickie from the side and studying her profile for many seconds before making his move. And Vickie takes the kiss coldly, not turning toward him more than a few degrees, not lifting her chin, not kissing him back. As a result Jake leans away and looks at her, wondering why she's so icy. Then very tactfully he approaches for another cheek kiss, again testing the waters, trying to find out whether Vickie likes being kissed or whether she feels annoyed by his forthrightness. Jake seems to realize that she's shy and that she's not going to do anything about returning the kiss because he slowly moves in and kisses her on the lips. In the space of about one minute he has gone from a first kiss on Vickie's cheek to a more intimate kiss on her lips, but Vickie hasn't turned toward him once or done more than stand there and receive his kisses. Nevertheless, these first two cheek kisses signal a very powerful change in their relationship. They are a turning point for Jake, signaling his commitment to Vickie, and despite her reticence they are also a turning point for Vickie, signaling her acceptance of Jake as her new boyfriend.

Of course not all cheek kisses need be done as deliberately or as slowly as in this scene. But when a cheek kiss is used as the first kiss a certain slowness and deliberateness can add to the kiss's impact. And since the recipient's lips are not usually touched in a cheek kiss, it's often a good idea to move from kissing the cheek to kissing the lips, as Jake finally does. The cheek kiss is not just a stepping stone to other kisses, though; it can signal tenderness and gentleness and be a wonderfully romantic way for lovers of any age or experience level to express their feelings.

The Cheek Kiss

A TENDER CHEEK KISS The first kiss Jake gives Vickie is a tender cheek kiss. Such a kiss can work as a first kiss between an experienced kisser like Jake and an inexperienced kisser like Vickie. A simple cheek kiss is much less likely to startle or frighten than a lip kiss or a French kiss.

WAITING FOR HER REACTION Jake waits in vain for a reaction from Vickie. She doesn't even turn her head to face him. Not sure what this means, but willing to be patient, he looks at her, apparently hoping for a return kiss.

ANOTHER CHEEK KISS When Vickie makes no move to return the kiss, Jake doesn't escalate things with a lip kiss; instead, he gives her another cheek kiss. Maybe Vickie likes this, maybe not. It's really hard to tell from her reaction.

MOVING TO THE LIPS Jake seems to interpret her lack of reaction as an invitation to kiss her lips, and he finally moves in that direction. Vickie can be seen opening her lips ever so slightly. She was receptive to Jake's tender cheek kisses and now appears ready for a lip kiss.

The Long Kiss

THE LONGER A KISS lasts, the more intimate it becomes, until at a certain point two kissers may feel that they've merged. In order to enjoy such a kiss, five things are necessary: a romantic setting, flirtatious preparation, proximity, correct breathing, and seductive hand action. All five elements can be found in the long kiss between Thomas Crown (Steve McQueen) and Vicki Anderson (Faye Dunaway) in *The Thomas Crown Affair* (1968).

Since most people don't kiss for more than sixty seconds at a time, a long kiss can be defined as any kiss in which lip contact extends beyond that one-minute mark. The best long kisses are those between people who are so drawn to each other that they can't bear to break apart. Such kisses often take place in a romantic setting. Millionaire Thomas Crown is entertaining insurance investigator Vicki Anderson at his mansion. During a game of chess, with a fire burning in the background, the setting says romance, and the game quickly heats up. Vicki flirts with the millionaire, who she suspects has robbed a bank. She seductively touches her lips, her arms, even the chess pieces themselves. This prepares both of them for the kiss and indicates that there's a romantic current running between them.

Another essential element of a long kiss is proximity. In this scene Thomas Crown seizes Vicki by the arm so that she finds herself face to face with the man she's been trying to implicate in a major bank robbery. The closeness of the two enables the kiss that follows to continue for over a minute. All their preliminary flirting still uppermost in their minds, they kiss with a depth of feeling that startles both of them, their bodies close from head to toe the entire time.

In order to prolong such a kiss it's necessary to breathe through the nose. Vicki and Thomas make this look easy. It's all right to break apart and take a few breaths now and then, but it's much more sophisticated to do what Vicki and Thomas do, namely, breathe through their noses. This allows them to enjoy more quality lip contact than would otherwise be possible.

Last but not least, proper hand movements are a prerequisite for an effective long kiss. Vicki wraps her arms around Thomas Crown's neck, figuratively encircling him with her charms. Throughout the entire kiss she keeps her hands moving caressingly and lovingly. Thomas Crown can also be seen moving one hand along her arm in a similar gesture. Their kiss has a highly charged eroticism that continues throughout its seventy-odd seconds of screen time. Remember, kissing techniques can't be copyrighted, and you too can use all the moves you've seen in *The Thomas Crown Affair* for your long kisses.

The Long Kiss

SETTING Millionaire Thomas Crown and insurance investigator Vicki Anderson play a game of chess during which more is at stake than winning. Games of any kind can prepare for a long kiss, especially when played in a romantic setting like this.

FLIRTING Vicki teases Thomas by seductively touching the chess pieces, her arms, and her lips. What man could resist? All these flirtatious images swirl around in his mind when the kiss begins, and they enable the kiss to continue unabated for a long time.

PREPARING Finally face to face, Vicki and Thomas have prepared themselves by being in a romantic setting, by maintaining eye contact, and by flirting.

BREATHING No long kiss can succeed without proper breathing. Here Vicki breathes through her nose. Proper hand action is also essential. Vicki wraps her arms around Thomas's neck in this breathtaking sequence.

The Risky Kiss

IN SOME SENSE every kiss is a risk since there's no guarantee that the kiss will be accepted. Risking a kiss, however, is often the only way to find true love, and a good example of how risking a kiss *can* lead to romantic love occurs in *Pretty Woman* (1990).

The scene is set in the evening after Vivian (Julia Roberts) and Edward (Richard Gere) have spent some time together. Vivian, who is a prostitute, has been warned by her friends never to kiss a man on the mouth because if she does she might fall in love. She has promised herself that she will not fall in love with Edward, a very successful businessman who has hired her to be his escort at some social events; instead, she plans to keep their relationship on a purely business level. But Edward has been so kind to her and so pleasant, and has helped her learn about so many of the finer things in life, that she has inadvertently come to admire him. In addition she finds him physically attractive. When he falls asleep one night, she approaches him and wonders whether she should go against her rules about not falling in love with the men she works with. To risk giving a kiss like this is naturally a difficult decision, which is why Vivian takes her time, trying to decide what to do. Eventually her feelings for Edward turn the tide in favor of taking the risk. The risk, of course, is twofold: first, that she'll fall in love with him, and second, that he won't return her feelings.

But true to her inner self, Vivian takes the chance and leans close, reaching out one hand as if approaching a dream that might vanish at any moment. In many ways Edward does represent a dream for her, the dream of true love and happiness. So she takes that chance and accepts the risk. At first, as if timid and uncertain about how he might react, she kisses him so lightly and softly that he doesn't even wake up. But after a few of these soft kisses, she apparently finds it hard to hold back and risks a more insistent kiss, with some pressure on the lips. When Edward blinks open his eyes and wakes up, he begins to return her romantic kisses with warmth and tenderness. The risk seems to pay off in this case. The kiss develops so effortlessly and so naturally for them both that it seems like Vivian has made the right choice. By the end of the film, of course, this is indeed the case. Risking a kiss in the right situation was for her the only way to find true love.

The Risky Kiss

FILLED WITH HOPE Vivian smiles down at Edward while he sleeps. Her heart is filled with the sudden hope that their relationship could develop into true love.

TAKING A RISK It would be a risk to kiss Edward because she doesn't know how he might respond, but perhaps the bigger risk is what the kiss might do to her heart. Vivian has always promised herself that she wouldn't fall in love with clients, but here she reaches out to take that risk.

BEING KISSED BACK Edward kisses back as tenderly and softly as Vivian, a sign that things are going in the right direction early in the kiss. But the risk continues: Vivian doesn't know how the kiss will affect her emotionally, and she's putting her heart on the line.

FEELINGS OF LOVE During the kiss, their entire professional relationship is changed and they find that they've awakened love and caring within themselves. Both are surprised and will need time to adjust to this new relationship.

The
Discovery
Kiss

WHEN A PERSON DISCOVERS something wonderful and heartwarming, the moment of recognition can be marked with one of the most life-changing kisses of all. A magical example of such a discovery kiss appears at the end of *You've Got Mail* (1998).

Joe (Tom Hanks) is a bookstore tycoon, and Kathleen (Meg Ryan) is the owner of a small bookstore that is being aggressively squeezed out of business by Joe and his large bookstore chain. They *should* hate each other, but on the Internet they have met and fallen in love—anonymously. The plot revolves around the fact that eventually Joe finds out the truth and starts to like Kathleen. In the last scene the truth is revealed, which leads to the discovery kiss.

The discovery takes place one fall afternoon in Central Park in an environment bursting with color, sunshine, and romance. Naturally their expectations are running high. When Kathleen sees Joe approaching she recognizes him at once as her business rival. Then suddenly she realizes that he is more than that—he is the man she has fallen in love with online, in fact he's the love of her life! She experiences a tremendous surge of feelings that brings her to tears. Of course she has mixed emotions, but underneath it all she's relieved and happy that Joe is the man she has fallen for.

She wanted it to be him all along, she says. This is a magical moment for her—she has discovered the truth and accepted it, and now she knows that they can be together as lovers, not as business rivals. Then they lean together for a discovery kiss. This is a recognition kiss for Kathleen because she has discovered who her online pen pal is. She had fallen in love with him over the Internet, and now she's falling in love with him all over again in person. The irony, of course, is that in real life she had disliked him so intensely because of his business practices.

This is a recognition kiss for Joe because he is finally able to reveal his identity to the woman he loves, and he's relieved to find that she loves him back just as much now as she did when they were only pen pals. In the twinkling of an eye their lives have changed for the better, and now that everything is in the open their kiss has tremendous meaning for both.

The change that occurs in their hearts is a discovery for Joe and Kathleen. They're renewed in a way that makes them happier and stronger because they've found their soul mates not only through e-mail but through their face-to-face meeting. The discovery kiss they share is the best way to deal with the emotions their experience has stirred up, and although it may have started out with a tear of confusion, by the end all those feelings have been transformed into tears of joy and happiness.

The Discovery Kiss

DISCOVERING THE TRUTH Kathleen has just discovered something potentially life-changing: The man she thought she hated is the man she really loves. In fact, she's had a loving pen-pal relationship with him all along. This is the best news she could have received, but also the most startling.

CALMING HER ANXIETY Joe calms her anxiety and reassures her that it is indeed true—he is the one who loves her, and he is the one who has been e-mailing her. Sometimes one partner needs to be reassured that the feelings are true.

FEELING THE CHANGE Both of them feel the change that's occurring to them at this moment. Kathleen is changed because she has found the love of her life in the most unlikely place, and Joe is changed because he can now be with the woman he loves without any pretense or disguise.

RECOGNIZING THEIR LOVE Having learned to trust their hearts, Kathleen and Joe let go of the past with a discovery kiss. They move into the kiss focusing not on their former feelings of competition but instead on their new feelings of love.

The Deciding Kiss

ONE OF THE MOST romantic kisses of all is the kiss that *decides* something between two people. It may come after weeks or months of agonizing conflict, romantic doubt, and confused feelings. The deciding kiss brings not only romance but relief into the hearts of the two who make it to the finish line. A good example of this kiss appears in *Bull Durham* (1988).

Annie (Susan Sarandon), a woman who loves baseball players, dallies with the hearts of two men throughout the film, but in the end she decides on one, and it is her deciding kiss that is the highlight of the story. It should be stressed that this kiss is slow and lingering. And how appropriate that this deciding kiss occurs after Crash (Kevin Costner) has told Annie: "I believe in long, slow, deep, soft, wet kisses that last three days." Their kiss simmers and sizzles, taking its time and promising to be romantic from the opening move where Annie softly kisses Crash on the side of the cheek, running her lips gently along his face.

They stand for a while without saying anything, simply keeping their heads together in a romantic pose. This pause in the middle of the kiss allows them to adjust to their new status as lovers. It allows Annie to realize that she has made her decision, that the other man is out and that Crash is her choice. It allows Crash the time to digest the fact that his rival has been vanquished and that *he* is number one in her heart. Their lingering embrace says a lot about how much they care for each other. That they have come through the uncertainties of a love triangle makes this moment poignant and their kiss quite meaningful. Annie runs her hand along his collar, her gesture saying that she loves him and that she's sure. This is the ultimate message of any deciding kiss.

Annie then puts one hand behind his head, caresses his hair, and smiles into his eyes. Their lips remain closed, but ever so slowly they draw closer together until at some point they both know a kiss is inevitable. When they do connect, there is passion and love in their slow but forceful kiss. The meaning of the kiss is evident in everything they do, from the careful way they move their heads back and forth, to the slowness of the kiss itself, to the fact that they keep their faces so close throughout, touching foreheads, cheeks, and noses and luxuriating in the contact. Their leisurely pace is a signal that they're not simply acting on impulse. Annie has made her choice after careful consideration, and this kiss confirms the fact—for both of them.

A deciding kiss is best done like this one in *Bull Durham*: slowly and carefully, allowing both partners to affirm that they've found a love they're sure will last.

The Deciding Kiss

THE CHOSEN ONE Crash is the chosen one and he's relieved that his rival has lost and he has won. He's now poised for a deciding kiss with the woman of his dreams.

MAKING A CHOICE Annie has put her heart on the line, loving two men, risking losing it all to find true love. But the way she gently kisses the side of Crash's face says she loves only him.

CONFIRMING THE CHOICE The choice is confirmed in these sweet caresses that punctuate the kiss, giving it duration, meaning, and timelessness. Actions like these speak louder than words, so Crash knows what she means—he's the only one in her heart.

SAYING IT ALL WITH A KISS The deciding kiss speaks for itself, confirming that they're two lucky people who've found true love. Incidentally, many women like to kiss a man who has some stubble, like Crash has in this scene. It gives him a rough and rugged bad-boy look that can be wonderfully exciting.

Tender Kisses

ONE OF THE KEYS to great kissing is achieving a degree of tenderness appropriate to the situation. While not *every* kiss needs to be tender and sweet—some are best when they're more passionate and aggressive—the majority of kisses can certainly benefit from some TLC. A great example of tenderness in kissing occurs in *The Locusts* (1997) with the kiss between Kitty (Ashley Judd) and Flyboy (Jeremy Davies), a naïve young man. Their kiss occurs during a picnic date.

The essence of tenderness is consideration for your partner, and in this scene consideration is everywhere, from the way they talk to each other to the way they look at each other, right down to the way they kiss.

Once Flyboy is on the date, he evokes sympathy by being his natural, rather simpleminded self. In contrast, the Ashley Judd character is much more experienced and worldly, and yet she connects with him because they have something in common: They're both outcasts. Flyboy is an outcast because he lives under the domination of his mother, and Kitty is an outcast because she's always running around with a new guy. In this scene, however, they connect as friends and then as romantic partners. During the short time they spend together they illustrate that true love can spring up in the most unlikely places.

The kiss begins while they're dancing to sentimental music from a portable radio, Kitty leading the rather clumsy Flyboy. Before long she gets close to him and discovers that, compared to the other boys she's gone out with, he has a certain natural, unaffected quality that appeals to her. While they're dancing close she looks at him and then puts her lips to his and kisses him gently and sweetly. She is clearly the initiator and Flyboy the recipient. The kiss takes them both by surprise, especially Kitty, and impulsively she kisses him again. When she suddenly realizes how bold and forward she's been it brings a smile to her lips. They stand in some embarrassment for a few moments, letting what just happened sink in. *Yes, I actually kissed him,* she seems to think, *and what's more, I enjoyed it.* In the seconds that follow the kiss, the tenderness of their interaction is emphasized by how little they say and do. Flyboy glances down as if he too is embarrassed and amazed by the whole experience.

Kissing with tenderness can be achieved by pressing gently and softly with the lips instead of hungrily and forcefully. Another element that adds to the tenderness in this scene is the empathy Kitty shows for the rather immature Flyboy and the consideration they have for each other. Physical softness and empathy can go a long way toward making your kisses as tender and sweet as this one from *The Locusts*.

Tender Kisses

FALLING IN LOVE Kitty surprises herself when she starts to fall in love with Flyboy, a socially inept boy who has not had many dates. This feeling of love is the beginning of the sequence that will lead to a very tender kiss.

DRAWN TOGETHER Flyboy and Kitty find themselves drawn together in a way neither could have imagined. Such is the nature of love that it can suddenly envelop two people in a feeling that will lead to a very special relationship.

SOFTNESS Because their relationship is so new, the kiss they exchange is incredibly soft and light. Notice that Kitty is not leaning her head forward even though she initiated the kiss.

LAUGHING IT OFF A tender kiss can release emotions and pent-up feelings, resulting in spontaneous laughter. Here Kitty and Flyboy are giggling at what just happened between them. Tender kissing is often some of the most powerful kissing.

The Goodbye Kiss

ALTHOUGH MANY PEOPLE routinely kiss those they love goodbye, few realize the full potential of this important kiss. It's rather simple to kiss someone goodbye, but it can be very powerful because it can keep you in your lover's heart until you meet again. An example of the proper technique for a goodbye kiss appears in *The Man Who Cried* (2000). The kiss occurs after Suzie (Christina Ricci) tells her lover, Cesar (Johnny Depp), that she intends to go to America to search for her father.

Everyone would agree that goodbye kisses have one overarching purpose: to tell the person you're leaving that you care deeply about them even though you're going away. So any goodbye kiss should contain passion despite the brevity of the kiss itself. The kiss between Suzie and Cesar has exactly the right amount of feeling at this crucial point, and their passion is apparent from the first moment to the last. The sequence opens with Suzie telling Cesar that she intends to go to America. She knows that he will remain in Europe and that they'll probably be separated forever.

This is a major goodbye, yet the technique used in their kiss can be copied by anyone, even if you're saying goodbye for only a short time.

The first thing that Suzie does is look at Cesar and say a few words. This is always a good way to begin because if you exchange endearments the kiss will be filled with positive emotions and love. Cesar then takes the initiative and puts his hand tenderly on Suzie's face. This move can also be copied to good effect since caressing your partner will tell them how much you care and that you wish you could return soon.

Finally Cesar and Suzie press their lips together with passion and feeling. This will probably be their last kiss, but their technique can be equally effective even if you're just going off to work for the day.

When all's said and done, saying goodbye with a kiss is really quite romantic. It's a sign of warmth and love that is almost required of lovers upon parting. Once they begin to kiss, Cesar and Suzie mash their lips together, taking their time and enjoying the kiss to the fullest. The key to an effective goodbye kiss is to convey your passionate love, leaving your partner with the feeling that you've got more to give and that they'll receive it when you return. The biggest mistake lovers make when saying goodbye is giving kisses that are tepid and chaste. By putting the same tenderness and feeling into your goodbye kisses as Cesar and Suzie, you'll say something your lover will not soon forget.

The Goodbye Kiss

REALIZING IT IS OVER Realizing that it's over, Cesar looks lovingly at Suzie. He knows that the best way to deal with this problem is to give a comforting goodbye kiss. The moment of parting can be stressful, but words and kisses can help bridge the gap that will open between lovers.

GENTLE CARESSES Cesar uses a gentle hand caress to begin his goodbye kiss, showing his affection and indicating that he still thinks the world of Suzie. This moment may live in their minds forever, so he makes it memorable by taking his time and being tender and loving.

LINGERING KISSES The sweetness of their goodbye kiss is enhanced by slow lip contact. They wish to get the last bit of pleasure from the moment, but more important they wish to express their undying love. This is the way to do a goodbye kiss, even if you're just going away for a short time.

FEELING THE LOVE Finally they hold each other, almost numb with the thought that they'll soon be separated. The proper end for a goodbye kiss is a hug or caress like this. Cesar's tears show how much he loves Suzie, and such tears are normal when a separation will be prolonged.

Promising with a Kiss

IN ADDITION TO COMMUNICATING affection and love, kisses serve to seal promises and assure lovers of devotion and commitment. A classic example of two lovers promising with a kiss occurs in *Jane Eyre* (1996). It's the first kiss between Jane (Charlotte Gainsbourg) and Mr. Rochester (William Hurt), her employer and, later in the story, her husband. Their kiss occurs outside on his estate one moonlit evening after Jane has returned from visiting a dying aunt.

The circumstances of making promises with a kiss vary, but they always have one element in common: both parties wish to show fidelity and faithfulness and to impress upon the other their absolute trustworthiness. In this scene they wish to assure each other of their commitment; however, the scene begins on a dissonant note with a discussion between the two based on misunderstanding and misinformation. Jane isn't happy with being treated like an inferior, an employee. There's also the problem of the beautiful Blanche Ingram looming in Jane's mind; she has suspected that Rochester is soon to become engaged to Blanche ever since she saw them together at a party. Rochester feels that he has always treated Jane as an equal, and he tells her that he's treating her as an equal now, kissing her gently on the cheek a number of times as if to prove he's sincere. But initially Jane doesn't kiss him back because she can't believe that he loves her. She has feelings for him but thinks he's playing with her mind. Rochester surprises the distraught Jane by telling her that it's *not* Blanche he loves. He confesses that he loves only *her.* "I love you as my own flesh," he says. "I beg of you to marry me. Say 'Edward, give me my name.' Say 'Edward, I will marry you.'" At this, Jane looks at him with mixed surprise and incredulous joy, almost disbelief. Can she have misjudged his heart so completely? Can he really love her, something she had hoped for but never really expected to happen?

Finally Jane lets her heart be her guide and she kisses Rochester back, promising to marry him. Her kiss is thoughtful and full of feeling, though she's still in shock from his confession of love. Jane's kiss is also a silent promise to marry Rochester and love him as he loves her. Her gentle caress is a sign of the affection she's now willing to reveal to the man she has been infatuated with all along.

Rochester kisses her tenderly and with passion, promising with his kiss to keep his word and love only her. Their exchange of kisses seals their engagement and goes further by saying that they love each other and always will. When lovers make promises as momentous as those made by Jane and Rochester, it's always appropriate to seal them with a kiss that communicates love and devotion.

Promising with a Kiss

TRYING TO ASSURE JANE Rochester tries to assure Jane that he's treating her as an equal, not as a mere employee. He does this first with words and with the sincerity of his voice.

INITIAL KISSES Rochester's initial kisses continue his attempt to assure Jane that he'll treat her as a loving partner, but it's hard for Jane to believe him because she still thinks he loves Blanche Ingram. Notice that she doesn't kiss him back at this point even though she's very much in love with him

REALIZATION Finally it dawns on Jane that Rochester really loves *her*, not Blanche. At this point she's ready to tell him of the deep feelings that she has kept hidden.

PROMISING Jane promises to love Rochester, and her tender kiss expresses her feelings better than words. In return he promises to marry her and love only her. Their exchange of promises and kisses demonstrates sincerity and affection and provides a perfect romantic conclusion to the scene.

The Reassuring Kiss

WHEN ONE PARTNER IS NERVOUS, uncertain, or experiencing anxiety, the considerate lover will be reassuring with a kiss that comforts and expresses love at the same time. Although words and caresses can also be comforting, sometimes a kiss is the most effective way to express your love and caring. A good example of how only a kiss will be reassuring in a particular relationship can be found in *Proof* (2005). The kiss occurs between Catherine (Gwyneth Paltrow), the daughter of a famous mathematician, and Hal (Jake Gyllenhaal), who is infatuated with her. They kiss one night after Hal has been drinking wine and talking with Catherine about her father, who is now deceased.

The fact that Catherine needs reassurance is not immediately apparent to Hal. In fact, he admits that he's slightly intoxicated and not exactly thinking clearly. He kisses Catherine quickly and impulsively. This first kiss is not premeditated but it expresses Hal's affection for Catherine. He tells her that he was always interested in her but restrained himself out of respect for her father, who was one of his teachers.

Hal's next kiss is sensitive and caring. Slowly but surely his kisses become more reassuring, and Catherine grows more receptive to them as they develop from impetuous and quick to slow and tender. This positive change in Hal's kissing style is what makes his later kisses more reassuring to her. It's important to note that his *feelings* haven't changed—he has always liked and cared for her—but his manner of *expressing* feelings through his kisses is what changes, and it changes for the better during the scene.

Hal's third kiss is even more tender and affectionate than his previous ones, and by this time Catherine knows that she feels something for Hal too. She tells him that she liked him when she saw him on campus. At this point Hal's kisses have reassured her that she's loved in return, and that Hal isn't merely acting on drunken impulse. Because Catherine suspects that she might be suffering from the same mental degeneration that afflicted her late father, Hal's kisses also reassure her that she can enjoy love despite her potential mental illness. In this sense, Hal's kisses are psychologically reassuring because of their tender and loving nature, which helps Catherine move toward a romantic relationship despite her fears.

Sometimes, for any number of reasons, a partner may need the reassurance of a loving, tender kiss. When those kisses are given as carefully and attentively as in this scene from *Proof,* they're sure to have the desired reassuring effect and express compassion, consideration, and true romantic love.

The Reassuring Kiss

IMPULSIVE Hal isn't initially reassuring, instead he's impulsive. His kiss, however, is the beginning of a series of kisses that will get better and better.

REASSURING His second kiss is more reassuring, careful, and attentive. Notice that he has his hand up to Catherine's side, gently caressing her face. This is a reassuring gesture which can help calm the anxieties of a partner who, like Catherine, is uncertain of many things in her life.

REASSURED Catherine slowly but surely becomes reassured because of Hal's attentiveness, his care in kissing her, and his kindness. This is exactly the medicine she needs at this point in their new relationship.

BETTER AND BETTER Hal's kisses get better and better as the scene progresses, developing into deep, soulful, reassuring kisses.

Kissing in the Snow

WHEN YOU NEED A REASON to celebrate, a place to have fun, or simply a moment to be a kid again, you can always kick back and kiss in the snow. The festive atmosphere and light-hearted spirit of kissing in the snow invariably makes it romantic and enjoyable. A wonderful example of this kiss appears at the end of *Bridget Jones's Diary* (2001) between Bridget (Renée Zellweger) and Mr. Darcy (Colin Firth), one of her boyfriends. Her other boyfriend (Hugh Grant) loses out to Mr. Darcy, and the kiss in the snow at the end of the film signals that the romance between Bridget and Mr. Darcy is the real thing.

The scene occurs at the end of the film because it's the culmination of a long search by Bridget for the perfect man. She wants someone she'll be compatible with, someone who cares for her, and above all someone who's sure that *she's* the one for *him*. All these things are what Mr. Darcy proves to be—by the *end* of the film. Based on Jane Austen's *Pride and Prejudice,* this Mr. Darcy starts out being a haughty snob who doesn't like Bridget.

By the end, however, everything gets sorted out, Mr. Darcy is revealed to be a sweetheart, and they're together at last, as they were always meant to be.

As they kiss, the falling snow embraces them like fairy dust. The swirling snow and beautiful surroundings increase their connection and ease their transition into romantic togetherness.

Kissing in the snow is different from kissing in any other environment, including water, rain, and wind. Nothing really compares to the sheer romance of this kiss. Rain, of course, is just too wet to be comfortable for long kissing sessions, although it can be romantic too and has been used in many films for a romantic effect. Wind has a disorienting quality and can be threatening at times. Water just can't compare to snow for pure romance and fun. Kissing in the snow provides a sheltered, private feeling. Any two people who kiss as these two do at the end of *Bridget Jones's Diary* are bound to feel some of the same delightful romantic energy.

Kissing in the Snow

SURROUNDED BY SNOWFLAKES When you kiss in the snow the beauty of nature will lift your spirits and inspire you. Notice that Mr. Darcy is looking at the snow and Bridget is looking at him. When kissing in the snow it's fun to take a break and enjoy the view.

ROMANCE IN THE AIR Snowflakes all around them, Bridget and Mr. Darcy are in a perfect environment for a romantic kiss. Sure, snow can be cold and wet, but the overall impression it makes on most lovers is positive and joyous.

USING THE ARMS Bridget wraps her arms around Mr. Darcy's neck, keeping him warm in the snow. A kiss in the snow can sometimes be done with fresh snowflakes on the lips, giving a cool burst of sensation that melts into the warmth of the kiss.

ENJOYING THE MOMENT Snow will eventually melt away, and perhaps this temporary quality makes enjoying it all the more urgent. Bridget and Mr. Darcy are getting every last ounce of pleasure possible from their encounter, and their slow approach is a perfect example of how to kiss in the snow.

Sunset Kisses

IF THERE'S ONE THING lovers the world over can agree on, it's that sunsets are romantic. A memorable example of a sunset kiss occurs in *The Majestic* (2001). The kiss occurs in a remote lighthouse, which adds to the romance.

The scene opens with Peter (Jim Carey) and Adele (Laurie Holden) going up into the lighthouse as the sun is dropping in the sky. Peter has amnesia and bears a striking resemblance to a World War II hero who Laurie was dating. She truly thinks he's her long-lost love—although he's not—and he believes her when she tells him that he's her boyfriend. Peter is trying to remember his former life, but in fact if he does remember his real past, Adele won't be his girlfriend. However, this is a perfect sentimental setup, and all the expectations of an amnesiac remembering are present as they get closer and closer for the kiss.

Adele is desperate to make him remember because she wants her boyfriend back, and Peter looks so much like her former lover that she mistakenly believes it's him. With the two of them in the remote lighthouse at sunset, the temptation is irresistible. It's such a perfect place for a kiss, and if they're ever going to jog his memory, *this* is the time to do it. With that in mind, Adele reaches out not only for Peter but for her long lost love, and she puts her hands behind his head and kisses him tenderly, longingly, and hopefully on the lips.

Peter kisses her back, and of course, not knowing who he really is, he's hoping he'll remember Adele being his girlfriend. No matter what the past was, he's falling in love with her all over again, and the funny thing is that she's falling in love with him too—the *new* Peter, the man who is here before her now. Memories mix into her feelings, the setting contributes to the romantic effect, and there is no doubt that she's in love with the man she is with—who, ironically, is not her long lost boyfriend, but a man who can't remember his identity.

The sunset kiss is full of tender and loving associations for lovers, just as the moonlight kiss is. The setting sun represents the force of nature going through its cycle. It represents life, love, and togetherness. Peter and Adele enjoy a sunset kiss, hoping that his memory will come back. What happens instead is that true love enlivens their hearts and warms their lives with its promise of a new beginning for them both.

Sunset Kisses

TRYING TO REMEMBER Peter is trying to remember who he is, but his amnesia is so complete that he can't even recall his name. The light of the setting sun on his face is symbolic of the need to act fast before it is too late. He feels pressure to remember.

HOPING TO HELP Adele hopes to help by kissing him. Perhaps the feel of a kiss will jog his memory. She is convinced that he is her boyfriend, and she believes a kiss might help them find the love she lost so many years ago. There is almost a look of desperation in her eyes as she moves in for the kiss.

KISSING AT SUNSET Romance is always present during a kiss at sunset. The forces of nature are on your side at this special moment. This is the time to kiss, and Adele and Peter feel the power of the sunset drawing them together.

SURROUNDED BY BEAUTY The sky is especially beautiful at sunset, and the beauty of nature can inspire beautiful and romantic kisses. Peter and Adele can't resist the appeal of this special time. Locations like this almost cry out for a romantic kiss.

Transforming Kisses

SOME KISSES HAVE the power to transform a relationship. Usually, but not always, these are first kisses. It pays to be on guard so that when such kisses occur, you'll fully enjoy their emotional power. One of the most famous transforming kisses occurs in *When Harry Met Sally* (1989) between two friends, Sally (Meg Ryan) and Harry (Billy Crystal). The film tells the story of how their friendship matures into love. The transforming kiss occurs one night when Harry tries to calm Sally down from an emotional upset. She cries and asks him to give her a hug to help her cope. When they hug, they're still friends. When *you* hug, you're still friends because hugs have nowhere near the power to transform a relationship that kisses do.

After the hug, Harry thinks it's all over. But Sally is still tearful, so Harry gives her a consolation kiss, a tiny little kiss. Be wary of consolation kisses, they can lead to more serious kisses. This little consolation kiss blossoms into a back-and-forth kiss that finds both of them giving and taking more than they bargained for. When your relationship progresses to this point, where you're *really* close friends, *and* you kiss on top of that, especially in an emotional state, things are never going to be the same. Their kiss is too deep, too soulful, too passionate to be anything other than a kiss of love. If you have a history of caring for someone who is "just a friend" and you take it to the next level, as Harry and Sally do, your kisses may have transformative power. Look at what happens next. We jump to later that night, and what's happened between them has put a big smile on Sally's face but a look of stupefied wonder on Harry's face. The key to getting through a transforming kiss is to realize that life is change—and sometimes two friends are going to become more than friends, sometimes they're going to fall in love. In the long run, the transforming kiss is really something to look forward to. If you're prepared for it, you'll come through with a big smile like Sally.

Transforming Kisses

HUGS Harry hugs his friend Sally. By the end of this exchange they're going to be more than simple friends. The power of a transforming kiss to change your life must be reckoned with.

CONSIDERATION Hugs and consolation are just the first step. When you let your feelings go, things can't remain the same.

BEFORE YOU KNOW IT . . . This kiss has gotten out of control—not that there's anything wrong with that! You've got to be prepared for the transformation that a kiss can make in your relationship.

TRANSFORMATION Sally is happy, Harry looks stunned. How could this have happened! Simple. It's those transforming kisses. And they can work the same magic for you.

PART TWO

The French Kiss and Other Advanced Kisses

The pleasures of trying a new technique are equaled only by the pleasures of seeing the reaction on your partner's face as you touch tongues, slide along her neck and arms with itsy-bitsy pecks, or lean her back for a Hollywood kiss. Perhaps you'd prefer a public kiss, a reclining kiss, or a candy kiss. If you like wilder things, experiment with ice-cream kisses, open-mouth kisses, even vacuum kisses. You can also indulge in the delightful Eskimo kiss, the blindfold kiss, or the victory kiss. For your kissing enjoyment, the following chapters offer up some of the trendiest and most *challenging* kisses around.

The
Open-Mouth
Kiss

NOT *ALL* open-mouth kisses are French kisses. Although French kisses involve tongue contact, some open-mouth kisses don't involve the tongue at all. You might find the open-mouth kiss appropriate when you wish to be close without becoming overly sexual. A good example of such a kiss appears in *Meet Joe Black* (1998). The scene begins with Joe (Brad Pitt) and Susan (Claire Forlani) getting ready for their first kiss. In this film Joe Black is the personification of Death, and, not surprisingly, he has very little experience with kissing. As a result, much of the action becomes Susan's responsibility. Since Susan is dealing with a beginner, she slows things down and takes her time. When you wish to do an open-mouth kiss it's advisable to move things along at a similarly slow pace so that your partner isn't misled into thinking you're heading for a French kiss. The leisurely tempo also gives you a chance to become creative and enjoy the unusual pleasures of the open-mouth kiss.

Susan kisses Joe's upper lip gently, and he reacts as if he's amazed by the whole experience. When you kiss a partner who has more experience than Joe Black, it's unlikely that he'll just stand there looking distracted, as Joe does. But the fact that you focus on the upper lip for a while is a good signal to your partner that you're going to dwell on the sensual aspects of the kiss. Next, Susan kisses his lower lip in a variation of lip-o-suction, a kiss in which partners alternately kiss the upper and lower lip. For your purposes, going from the upper to the lower lip is a good idea because it adds variety to the kiss. Ultimately this gives Joe a few ideas of his own and he kisses *her* lower lip too, playfully nipping it between his lips and tugging on it. All this time their mouths are slightly open.

Sometimes, introducing an artificial constraint—like doing an open-mouth kiss with no tongue—can foster creativity. Because no tongue is used in this scene, Susan and Joe become creative and take their time with the open-mouth kiss.

The Open-Mouth Kiss

SLOWER Susan looks at Joe Black and decides to slow things down by kissing at a beginner's pace. Sometimes it's nice to regress and become a neophyte again. You can use the same slow strategy to get more fun out of your kisses.

UPPER First she kisses his upper lip. Hopefully, your partner won't look so distracted.

LOWER . . . Then she goes for his lower lip.

OPEN-MOUTH Finally Joe gets the idea and kisses her back, focusing on her lower lip. Notice that both have their mouths slightly open but no tongue is involved. Before long Joe Black is breathing new life into the open-mouth kiss, nipping his partner's lower lip and tugging on it. Try this next time you want to slow things down and heat things up.

The French Kiss

THE MOVIE *Cry-Baby* (1990) provided director John Waters with a number of opportunities to satirize the teen movie genre. One of the ways he does this is to include explicit French kisses that show the use of the tongue much more graphically than we usually see in romantic movies. Several sequences show a group of boys and girls French kissing on a dance floor. Another sequence shows teenagers making out and French kissing in a field at night. But the key scene illustrating the French kiss occurs when Cry-Baby (Johnny Depp) convinces Allison (Amy Locane) to French kiss in the park. "It's easy," he says. "You just open your mouth, and I open my mouth, stick out your tongue, and kiss."

You might want to try some of the techniques that Cry-Baby uses when kissing his partner. First, he tells her that they're going to do a French kiss. You could tell your partner what you're up to if she's totally clueless, like Allison, but most girls would find it awkward if you announced that you were going to use your tongue. Better to move right on to his next technique: He opens his mouth and leans close. By opening your mouth and leaning close you encourage your partner to do the same. Finally, he uses a few advanced French kissing techniques. For example, he rotates his tongue around Allison's tongue. You can clearly see how this is done in this scene. Next, he sucks her tongue from the middle right down to the very tip of her tongue. By using this technique you'll avoid the back of your partner's mouth, which is very important because she has to be able to breathe through the entire kiss. And by occasionally sucking the tongue you'll excite her and show that you're a creative kisser. Using these French kissing techniques, you too can kiss like a Hollywood leading man. And if your partner comments that you kiss like Johnny Depp, how can you complain?

The French Kiss

TALK Cry-Baby is talking about what he's planning to do so that Allison, who's not an experienced kisser, isn't totally surprised when the tongues come into play.

TONGUE The next step in the French kiss is the use of the tongue. Cry-Baby's eyes are open so that he can see what he's doing.

TOUCH The contact of two tongues allows for a lot of creativity. During this French kiss Cry-Baby and Allison roll their tongues around each other's. In this frame Cry-Baby's tongue is on top.

TECHNIQUE An advanced technique, not often seen in movies, involves sucking your partner's tongue.

The
Flicking Kiss

ADVANCED FRENCH KISSES can involve many actions, but probably none as important as flicking the tongues. Unfortunately, there aren't many film examples of this technique because it usually happens inside the mouth, but the kiss does occur in visible form in James Toback's *Two Girls and a Guy* (1997). Carla (Heather Graham) is kissing Blake (Robert Downey Jr.). At one point Carla and Blake retire into a loft and kiss. The camera comes in for a close-up view of the French kiss, which involves lots of tongue contact. Blake uses a flicking action, but instead of keeping his tongue in his partner's mouth, he pushes it all the way out of his mouth. In most cases, you'll be doing this flicking motion inside your partner's mouth, just touching the tip of your partner's tongue. For the purposes of the film, however, the actors and director probably decided on a more exterior kind of French kiss so that the audience could see what was happening. As Blake moves his tongue up, Carla simultaneously sticks her tongue out and begins to flick her tongue up also. Once Blake reaches

Carla's upper lip, he brings his tongue back down, reversing his previous action, and on the way down he meets Carla's tongue again. Because of the extreme flexibility of the tongue muscles, this flicking of the tongues can also be done side-to-side or in a rotating motion, an action that can be repeated many times for good effect. It's important to note that in most instances it's just the tips of the tongues that are flicked together. Think of what a snake does with its tongue and you'll get the idea. The tempo in this film varies from slow to medium, but when you try it you can use a rapid-fire flicking action, which is considerably faster than the one used here. As mentioned, this technique works best inside the mouth, but you can certainly try an exterior version just like these two for an equally delightful effect.

The Flicking Kiss

GENTLY MOVING UP Blake begins with his tongue touching Carla's lower lip.

LOSING CONTACT He flicks upward gingerly. At the same time, she begins to move her tongue out of her mouth and up, as if trying to catch his. Notice that when flicking the tongues it's normal to occasionally lose contact with your partner's tongue.

REPEATING THE ACTION Flicking is a joyful technique when done properly. The key is to get a rhythm going and stay in the front of the mouth.

INTIMACY AND TECHNIQUE Carla is jealous, which may be why she's kissing so erotically. Flicking the tongues can win a partner back to you because of the closeness it fosters. Indeed, flicking the tongues is one of the most intimate and erotic kissing techniques.

The Eskimo Kiss

THE MOVIE *Sabrina* (1954) is about a young debutante (Audrey Hepburn) and the two brothers she loves. In the course of the story she comes home and dances with the younger brother, David Larrabee (William Holden), a playboy who hasn't seen her in two years. Finding her totally changed and irresistible, he forgets all about his fiancée and wants nothing more than to be with Sabrina. As they dance together they enter a world of romance and share a cheerful Eskimo kiss. Although this kiss is often considered childish, it can actually be quite erotic.

The scene begins with Sabrina and David dancing, which naturally brings romance into the picture. As if that weren't enough, he's entranced by her beauty, and she reveals that she once had a secret crush on him. For a while thereafter they dance close and gaze into each other's eyes, building romantic tension.

Before long they're heart-to-heart, holding each other close and revealing things about themselves that you only reveal to the one you love. This preliminary interchange precedes the kiss and creates a romantic atmosphere. When you anticipate doing an Eskimo kiss, it's always a good idea to build loving tension with plenty of eye contact and flirtatious banter.

Next the couple dances cheek to cheek. This is a novel way to do an Eskimo kiss, which usually involves running your nose along your partner's or, in some variations, simply rubbing your cheeks together. This kind of Eskimo kiss is clearly not for children. It certainly takes a bit of willpower to resist touching lips to lips when you're already this close, but resisting the urge will keep the kiss romantic and tantalizing, as it is for these two.

Face to face is the name of the game, and Sabrina and David don't hesitate to get close and stay close while dancing. The payoff is obvious in Sabrina's smile. This kiss is hard to top, for without any lip contact at all it can cement a relationship and make you feel right at home with your new lover. Perhaps the only thing this sequence omits is the rubbing of the noses typical of many Eskimo kisses. But, as Sabrina and David demonstrate in this scene, nose rubbing isn't essential for an Eskimo kiss, simply dancing cheek to cheek is enough to make temperatures rise and pulses race.

The Eskimo Kiss

DANCING TOGETHER Sabrina and playboy David Larrabee dance the night away and seem to fall in love with each other after a two-year absence during which Sabrina has blossomed into an irresistible beauty. Eye to eye, they begin to think about spending the rest of their lives together.

GETTING CLOSE Finally dancing cheek to cheek, they're doing what many Eskimos do when they kiss—pressing their cheeks together. From this position you can actually carry on a conversation, provided, of course, that you talk *only* of love.

LOOKING IN OPPOSITE DIRECTIONS An Eskimo kiss often winds up like this, face to face. It can also help to smack your lips, without touching mouth to mouth, inhaling the hopefully delicious fragrance of your partner.

CONTINUING THE ESKIMO KISS Although often considered childish, you'll never see children kiss quite like this. An Eskimo kiss is hard to top for romance.

The Candy Kiss

THE SWEETNESS and surprise of a candy kiss are pleasures every lover deserves. A beautiful example of the candy kiss appears in the film *Wide Sargasso Sea* (1993). Antoinette (Karina Lombard) is in bed with her husband (Nathaniel Parker), and she's eating grapes. At the same time she's sitting on top of him and carrying on a conversation. These two points suggest that when doing your own candy kisses you needn't actually use candy. Although many people like to pass mints, Lifesavers, or other hard candy mouth to mouth, the kiss works just as well with grapes, blueberries, or any small fruit. It helps to be close to your partner, especially if you plan to surprise him. Having a conversation is a great cover for your surreptitious actions in sneaking a piece of candy into your mouth so that you can pass it to him during a kiss. In this scene, however, Antoinette gives Edward fair warning, asking him to close his eyes and open his mouth. He's delighted with the whole idea and complies with her request. If you intend to surprise your partner, some diversionary tactics may be called for so that he doesn't know what you're doing.

Antoinette then leans down over Edward and kisses him. In doing your own candy kisses, you may wish to kiss once or twice before passing anything to your partner because this will pave the way for fun and provide a sensory contrast to the feel and taste of the candy he'll be receiving. After she kisses him, Antoinette transfers the grape from her mouth to his. If this is a surprise candy kiss, your partner will usually react with glee or some mixture of confusion and amazement. Whether it's a surprise or not, you're sure to get a reaction to this kiss.

The Candy Kiss

SWEET FRUIT Antoinette dangles grapes before her husband. He doesn't seem too enthused. Don't let a bad sport stop you from doing a candy kiss now and then.

SWEET TALK If your partner is less than enthusiastic, sweet-talk him into trying a candy kiss. Antoinette tells Edward to close his eyes and open his mouth.

SWEET-TEMPERED A sweet-tempered partner is a joy, especially when you plan to spring a candy kiss on him.

SWEET LIFE Life may be a bowl of cherries, but a candy kiss works just as well with a Lifesaver. Here Antoinette transfers a grape to Edward. Remember to kiss once or twice before you pass the candy. The candy kiss can also lead to some very intimate follow-up kisses, so it's definitely worth a try.

The
Sliding Kiss

MANY YOUNG MEN wonder *where* they should kiss their partner to please her best, but since the spot varies from woman to woman, the best way to find it is to observe her while doing a sliding kiss. A sliding kiss, as its name implies, involves executing a series of little pecks along your partner's legs, arms, or any other part of the body that isn't covered by clothes. A good example of this kiss appears in *Dirty Dancing* (1987) when novice dancer Baby (Jennifer Grey) is kissed by Johnny (Patrick Swayze), her dance instructor and lover.

The first spot you kiss for a sliding kiss is rather significant: it's the starting point for your kissing journey, and if you choose the spot carefully, your sliding kisses will last longer and have greater impact. Johnny makes his choice carefully, looking at Baby's neck before committing himself to any particular point along it. When he does move down to plant the first kiss, it's very low on the neck, an excellent choice because this spot allows him to travel much further than if he had started immediately under the jaw, for example, or directly on her chin. By selecting an appropriate starting point, he gives his partner a hint of what's to come and subtly suggests to her that there's much more on the way in the form of sliding kisses. And he delivers on this unstated promise by sliding up along Baby's neck, executing tiny little kisses as he goes. Continuing in this way, he makes progress up the neck, planting little kisses as he moves higher. This same technique can be employed to good effect along the arm, the leg, and the back; indeed, anywhere that might please your partner is fair game for a sliding kiss.

The problem with some sliding kisses, unfortunately, is that while doing them you might not be able to see your partner's reaction. But since seeing the kissee's reaction is such a crucial part of a sliding kiss, it's worth taking a break every now and then to slow down and watch her, as Johnny does. In other words, he doesn't get so involved in the kiss that he forgets to look to see how Baby is reacting. In most cases, of course, you'll be able to see just how she likes, or dislikes, each spot you kiss. But if you start on her ankle or low on her neck, it might be difficult to observe how she's taking the kiss, and pausing to look at her, as Johnny does here, is the best solution to this problem. Another reason to watch your partner while doing a sliding kiss is that if you get a good reaction, like Johnny does with Baby, you'll know *that's* the spot to kiss next time.

The Sliding Kiss

PREPARING TO SLIDE Before commencing his sliding kiss, Johnny takes the time to choose a spot to start. Don't hesitate to inspect your partner like this before planting your first kiss.

THE FIRST KISS Once he has decided to start low, Johnny wastes no time and moves right in for a first kiss on Baby's neck. Sometimes you'll get lucky and the first spot you touch will really excite your partner, but if not you can slide along to other spots, as Johnny is doing here, planting itsy-bitsy kisses along the way.

SLIDING UP A sliding kiss is one of the most creative things you can do with your lips because there are so many different areas you can slide to and so many different ways you can kiss as you move along. Johnny moves up the neck, cupping his hands around Baby's shoulders for support.

TINY PECKS ALONG THE WAY The sensual aspect of a sliding kiss is illustrated nicely in this frame where Baby moves her head up in response to the sliding kiss Johnny has given along her neck. The more little kisses he gives her, the more she seems to enjoy it.

The Hand Kiss

ONE OF THE MOST interesting and, incidentally, most romantic, if you can believe it, hand kisses on film occurs in the opening minutes of David Gordon Green's *All the Real Girls* (2003). Hand kisses are unusual in the West although they do survive as a formal and courtly method of greeting in some European countries, especially Poland, where men may be seen bringing their lips close to a woman's hand (though not actually touching it with their lips) when meeting and greeting. But the hand kiss in this movie speaks volumes about the erotic potential of the lost art of kissing the hand. The film tells the story of a boy, Paul (Paul Schneider), who falls in love with his friend's sister, Noel (Zooey Deschanel). One night Paul is standing with Noel when the subject of kissing comes up. It's sometimes awkward to talk about a kiss before it happens, but there *are* exceptions and this is clearly one of them. Noel suggests that if Paul wishes to kiss her differently from all the other girls he's kissed, he should kiss her hand. And then she holds out her hand, palm up. In and of itself this doesn't sound too romantic, but when looked at in context it actually comes across as brilliant and sweet, in large part because Paul, mad romantic that he is, seriously considers the prospect of kissing her hand. He asks her ex*act*ly where she wants the kiss, and Noel points to the precise spot in the palm of her hand that she has in mind. Paul goes on to do some funny things before he kisses Noel's hand. First he brushes it off to clean it, then he blows on it, perhaps to jokingly clean it off a bit more before his lips touch it. Actually, everything he's doing has great erotic potential, and if you think a hand couldn't possibly be erotic, just watch this movie. It turns out that the hand, having more nerves than almost any other part of the body, is ex*trem*ely sensitive, especially the thumb, the index finger, and, yes, the palm. Paul makes excellent use of this curious fact, taking his time, holding Noel's hand, and finally lowering his lips to it for a wonderfully long kiss directly on her palm. Of course, this being a romance, that hand kiss leads to another kind of kiss. The point to be stressed here is that a hand kiss has more erotic potential than most people believe, and if you take your time and do it creatively, as in this sequence, you'll certainly emerge from the experience a hands-down winner.

The Hand Kiss

PALMS UP Paul and Noel are talking about kissing when she suggests he kiss her hand. You can use the same kind of creative thinking to make your partner stop and take notice. Is she serious? Once Paul realizes that she *is* serious, he gets creative himself.

HANDY MAN Noel points to exactly the spot she wants kissed. The way a man kisses a hand says a lot about how he'll act as a lover. Hopefully, he'll take his time and do it right.

BLOWN AWAY Paul has a comic side, brushing Noel's hand and blowing to clean it off. If you can make a girl laugh she'll fall in love with you.

FROM HAND TO LIPS Despite how sensitive they are, hands have only so much romantic potential. Eventually your hand kisses will lead to more intimate lip kisses, as they do for Paul and Noel.

The Hollywood Kiss

ONE OF THE MOST FAMOUS movie kisses of all time is the kiss in *Gone With the Wind* (1939) at the foot of the staircase. Rhett Butler (Clark Gable) catches up with Scarlett O'Hara (Vivien Leigh) and leans her back for a passionate kiss. You can easily use Rhett's technique once you understand the secret of the Hollywood kiss. (The name itself comes from the fact that the kiss looks so good that many directors incorporate some version of it in their films.)

All the essential moves for a Hollywood kiss can be learned from watching this one classic scene. First, Rhett catches up with Scarlett at the foot of the staircase. He uses his left hand to seize her arm and spin her around to face him. If you start your own Hollywood kisses by making sure your partner is facing you, you'll have the same success Clark Gable had with this memorable kiss.

The next thing that happens in any good Hollywood kiss is that the initiator of the kiss puts his hands around the waist of the person to be kissed. When Rhett grabs Scarlett around the waist and looks into her eyes, something very important occurs. Scarlett discovers that their recent argument has not stopped him from having strong feelings for her. Somewhat confused by the mixed messages she's been receiving from him, she's caught off guard by his sudden ardor. In most cases when a man leans a woman back for a Hollywood kiss, she can decide whether to assist the kisser or move away and prevent the kiss from happening. In this case, Scarlett instinctively leans back, letting Rhett lead her into the next phase of the kiss.

What made the Hollywood kiss so memorable in *Gone With the Wind* was that Scarlett loved Rhett but was confused by him. She never knew whether he really loved her back. In real life, your partner will probably not be as confusing and unpredictable as Rhett Butler. When he leans you back you may at first be startled, but if you respond correctly, you can help him execute the kiss with flair and grace.

In the final stage of the kiss, Rhett leans Scarlett back at an angle and kisses her passionately on the lips. The secret to getting a cooperative partner for a Hollywood kiss is making her feel safe when you lean her back. To that end, you must keep your hands securely around her waist, as Rhett does with Scarlett, so that she has some support. It's also essential to make sure that she doesn't topple over and fall, and the way to do that is to keep your *own* balance throughout the kiss, as Rhett does by standing with his weight equally divided on both feet. When you try this one, maintain your balance and stay in control, and your Hollywood kisses will be as memorable—and also as beautiful—as the most famous kiss in *Gone With the Wind*.

The Hollywood Kiss

CATCHING In *Gone With the Wind* Rhett catches Scarlett at the bottom of the staircase and turns her around to face him.

HOLDING Once they're face-to-face, he puts his arms around her back. This does two things: It signals that a kiss is imminent and it serves to support her in the next, crucial phase of the kiss.

LEANING Although Scarlett resists Rhett, your partner will hopefully not be as feisty when you lean her back. The fact that his hands are firmly around her waist prevents her escape and also communicates the message that he's not going to let her fall.

KISSING Leaning her straight back—not to one side or the other—Rhett kisses Scarlett passionately. The trick to doing a Hollywood kiss is really having a cooperative partner. By the end of this kiss Scarlett is once again won over by Rhett, and the scene ends with him carrying her up the stairs.

The Messy Kiss

A VERY CREATIVE example of the messy kiss occurs in the opening moments of *Ghost* (1990). The scene begins as Molly (Demi Moore) is working on her pottery wheel. Her lover, Sam (Patrick Swayze), gets behind her and starts playing with the wet clay. This is messy by any standards, but above all it's sexy. Molly doesn't seem to mind Sam's playful interruption, in fact she appears to welcome it. The key to enjoying messy kisses is to find a time and place to get down and dirty together. Some couples like to pass candies back and forth or lick chocolate off a cake and then lick it off each other's fingers and tongue. Anything along these lines will get you into the realm of the messy kiss.

Next, Sam gets even closer, putting his head alongside Molly's. By copying or mirroring your partner's physical position, for example by sitting facing the same direction or by adopting her body position yourself, you create rapport. Very soon things heat up even more as Sam kisses her ear. His hands covered in the wet clay, he's caressing her and kissing her at the same time. This kind of tactile stimulation is playful and erotic if you take it nice and slow and build up to it, as Molly and Sam do in this scene. That way, you'll both have similar expectations about the messy kiss. It might also help to have a few towels handy!

Before long Sam and Molly are getting distracted, and the messy kiss continues unabated with Sam kissing Molly and then hugging her with his clayey hands. The secret to enjoying this kind of kiss is recapturing the childish joy of letting go and not caring about getting dirty. This scene from *Ghost* offers a significant message for all lovers: A messy kiss can be a sexy kiss, and that's something worth remembering.

The Messy Kiss

GETTING MESSY Sam isn't afraid to get messy with Molly. Sitting behind her, he plays with the wet clay—and with her—thoroughly enjoying himself. The key to messy kisses is to let your inhibitions go and become playful and frisky.

GETTING CLOSE An excellent technique for any lover is to face the same direction as your partner. Sam and Molly are looking the same way, sitting cheek to cheek. This fundamental romantic position can increase feelings of togetherness and build rapport.

GETTING HOT Sam heats things up by kissing Molly's ear. When you're facing the same direction, all it takes is a slight turn of the head to make things romantic.

GETTING DISTRACTED Their hands wet with pottery clay, Molly and Sam continue kissing. All the messy playing seems to have loosened up their inhibitions. On a more mundane level, you could try washing the dishes together or frolicking on a sandy beach while kissing for a similar effect.

The Blindfold Kiss

GAMES, GAMES, GAMES. Every lover plays them, and one of the most enjoyable kissing games is kissing with a blindfold. This kiss appears in a particularly sensual form in *Mostly Martha* (2001). The idea behind a blindfold kiss is that the kiss has a fun element of mystery. In effect, it's a mind game, but it can have sweet consequences for both the blindfolded partner and the one who can see.

The kiss begins when an Italian chef, Mario (Sergio Castellitto), comes to visit another chef, Martha (Martina Gedeck). The two have been fighting and flirting, as is usual in any romantic comedy, and this is the point where they make their breakthrough into a full-fledged romantic relationship. Mario has brought a pot of soup for Martha to taste, and they play a game with her being blindfolded during the taste test. He spoon-feeds Martha, and it's her job to try to guess the ingredients without looking. For your own experiments, the blindfold will serve a similar purpose in increasing the tactile sensations of the sightless person. At the same time, the one who can see will enjoy a dominant advantage simply because the other is temporarily blinded. This adds another erotic dynamic to the kiss.

The game progresses as Mario continues to feed spoonfuls of soup to Martha. You can use the same game plan, feeding fruit, berries, or even candy to your blindfolded partner. In each case, she has to guess what the item is. Sometimes it's hard to tell without looking. This part of the game will heighten her tactile and auditory senses and prepare her for the kisses to follow.

Mario doesn't tell Martha that he's going to kiss her. He simply hesitates with the last spoonful and then sips the soup himself. When the time is ripe, without any warning, lean toward your blindfolded partner and approach for the kiss. If you do it slowly enough, the approach phase will almost always alert her that a kiss is imminent. She can feel the heat from your face, hear the sounds of your approach, or in other nonvisual ways sense that you're getting closer. Most important, she'll feel a sense of anticipation that will heighten the pleasure of the kiss when your lips finally connect.

Mario kisses Martha tenderly and gently, and she gets to enjoy the thrill of a kiss in the dark. But this game works both ways. The kisser also gets a certain thrill from kissing a blindfolded person because in his imagination she could be anyone he'd like to fantasize about. The game continues even when the blindfold comes off. Now that they've experienced kissing with it on, the kisses that follow have a certain special quality, calling to mind the experience both partners just had. At this point it's time to reverse roles and let the other partner wear the blindfold.

The Blindfold Kiss

THE BLINDFOLD Martha is wearing a blindfold. This heightens tactile sensation for the person who can't see. At the same time, it lets the person who *can* see fantasize that he's about to kiss someone else, a stranger perhaps or someone supremely sexy and exciting.

THE GAME Mario feeds soup to Martha, who has to guess the ingredients. The game rules can be changed easily enough. Feed your partner chocolates for a fun variation. Or dispense with the food altogether and go right into the kiss.

THE APPROACH Mario approaches very slowly, which increases anticipation. Your blindfolded partner will sense your approach by the feel of the heat from your face, the soft rustling sounds of your clothes, and other subtle sensual hints.

THE KISS The kiss itself is a fantasy for both Mario and Martha. She feels it more intensely because she can't see, and he feels in control because he can. Your own blindfold kisses will almost certainly leave you wanting more, either with or without the prop.

The
Public Kiss

ALMOST EVERYONE LIKES to kiss in public occasionally because it shows the world you're a couple. The public kiss in *Top Gun* (1986) between Maverick (Tom Cruise) and Charlie (Kelly McGillis) illustrates the technique perfectly. As in this scene, any good public kiss will have some element of privacy as well as some element of visibility to others. In addition, a good public kiss will be memorable if it takes place in a nice location, like this one at dockside.

One of the reasons it's advisable to have some element of privacy, even during a public kiss, is to make sure that the two of you feel comfortable. When Maverick and Charlie kiss in this scene, other people *are* present, though not close enough to interfere. By stopping his motorcycle at the side of the dock, Maverick puts them in a place where they're not likely to be disturbed. When planning your public kisses, keep this element of privacy in mind because it can contribute substantially to your enjoyment of the experience. A key reason Maverick and Charlie seem to enjoy their public kiss so much is that the only other people present are quite far away. Your public kisses need not have such a complete element of privacy as in this case: Simply going under a tree in a park or out on a rowboat will usually be enough to give you the comfort and privacy you need.

Maverick and Charlie kiss on the motorcycle while a ship passes in the background, but they don't turn around to look, they stay focused on the kiss. This is the proper technique; there's really no need to look at others who are present, especially when they're so far away. Before long a very intimate kiss is developing, with Charlie kissing Maverick's lower lip and tugging it gently. The intimacy of a public kiss can vary widely, from a quick peck all the way to a more intimate French kiss. As a general guideline, it's safe to say that the further away people are, the more intimate your kisses can become. Maverick and Charlie's kiss nicely illustrates how intimate a public display of affection can become when done in a rather isolated spot, with Maverick using his tongue to get in a quick French kiss. By taking note of the techniques used in this scene from *Top Gun,* you'll be able to make all your public kisses pleasantly exciting.

The Public Kiss

SELECTING A LOCATION Maverick selects a dock for his public kiss with his teacher, Charlie. If the location is aesthetically pleasing it can make a public kiss memorable.

KISSING IN PUBLIC Every public kiss demands some degree of concentration from the participants, which is one reason it can be so much fun. You've got to block out the world and any onlookers while you focus on your partner. Maverick and Charlie seem to have blocked out everyone and everything.

SHOWING OFF On some level we're all exhibitionists, and one of the pleasures of kissing in public is being seen together doing something like this. Here, Maverick and Charlie demonstrate their affection for the world to see, oblivious to the consequences of being seen.

The Reclining Kiss

THE DYNAMICS OF kissing can change considerably when lovers are lying down. If they're side by side they can kiss at will in a relaxed position. If one is over the other, the one on top can have more control over the kissing tempo, while the one on the bottom can enjoy receiving rather than initiating most of the kisses. A very enjoyable kissing position indeed is the reclining kiss, and a good example of it appears in *City of Angels* (1998).

Maggie (Meg Ryan) is a doctor who falls in love with Seth, an angel (Nicolas Cage). As our scene opens he's injured his lip and is lying down, being tended to by Maggie, who is lying beside him in front of the fireplace. Actually this is a good example of a position that you can incorporate into your kissing strategy. Use any excuse to get into a reclining position with your partner because this will afford you plenty of opportunities for the reclining kiss.

Maggie props herself up on one arm and inclines her head over the patient. This is another technique that should be easy to copy. Once you're lying side by side, it helps if one of you takes the initiative, like Maggie does here, perhaps propping yourself up on one elbow to get close and ready for the kiss. Do it slowly so that you don't accidentally fall onto your partner. Maggie takes her time, and all the while her patient is looking up into her eyes, ready for her next move.

As Maggie leans down, Seth raises his hands and caresses her face, guiding her toward him. At this point they're intertwined nicely and each one is ready for the reclining kiss. She's leaning down toward him and he's waiting for the kiss. When reclining, use the same strategy if you're on top, leaning close to your partner. If you're on the bottom, be patient and let your partner control the direction and timing of the action.

Shortly after they make lip contact, Maggie rolls over onto her side and looks lovingly at Seth. During a reclining kiss it isn't necessary to kiss during the entire time that you're lying together. Now and then you can become slightly separated. The very fact that you're still close should be enough to keep the romance alive so that at any moment you can get back to kissing or caressing. Eventually Maggie rolls onto her back, and Seth takes a more active role, leaning over her for the continuation of the kiss. Once you become comfortable with this position, you can take turns being the initiator and the receiver, exploring all the romantic possibilities of the reclining kiss.

The Reclining Kiss

RECLINED Maggie and Seth are lying side by side and she's gazing affectionately at him. Once you find yourself in this position, you'll have more than caregiving on your mind too.

INCLINED TO KISS Maggie takes the superior position while Seth looks up at her with a certain haggard anticipation. Getting set for your own reclining kisses may involve propping yourself up on one elbow.

MOVING IN Here's where the fun really starts. She's coming down for the kiss, and he's guiding her in for the landing. If you don't kiss after getting intertwined like this, you're missing the point.

BACK TO THE RECLINING KISS Now Seth reverses roles and initiates a reclining kiss with Maggie. She doesn't seem to mind. And neither will you when you try a reclining kiss of your own.

The Aggressive Kiss

MANY WOMEN FEEL that it's a man's job to be the aggressor and initiate a kiss, especially a first kiss. In our society most men feel the same way. There are times, however, when a woman needs to take the first step. This can be because the man is shy, inexperienced, or, as in the case of Harry Morgan in *To Have and Have Not* (1944), just plain reticent. Whatever the reason, every woman needs to know how to get things moving by using the aggressive kiss.

In this famous scene, Slim (Lauren Bacall) is teasing Morgan (Humphrey Bogart). During the filming of *To Have and Have Not* the two fell in love in real life, and the chemistry between them is obvious. Because Morgan is a man who likes to mind his own business, even his relations with women are less aggressive than usual. So it's up to Slim to get things going, and she does this by taunting Morgan verbally. You can use the same tactics if you want to initiate a kiss with a man. Tease him and adopt a flirtatious attitude because that might get him interested. If not, proceed on to phase two, as Slim is forced to do here when Morgan doesn't take the bait.

In phase two, since her taunting didn't have the desired result, she actually sits on his lap, invading his personal space. Only try this with a guy you're very friendly with. Most men would consider it a compliment if a girl they liked sat on their knees like this, and Morgan reacts as expected. He likes it, but he continues to act standoffish, forcing Slim to proceed to phase three.

Her next tactic is the classic get-close-and-make-eye-contact move. Sitting on his lap, her hands on his chest, her face just inches from his, Slim continues to be the aggressor, working her way up to the kiss itself. When Morgan still doesn't make a move, she does. In the final phase of her approach, she plants one on him. Bogart, naturally, takes it like a man. He simply sits there and lets her kiss him. If your man reacts the same way, give him another kiss, as Slim does with Morgan. Then she gets up and, in a sultry drawl, says: "It's even better when you help."

No woman should be without the aggressive kiss in her arsenal of smooches. Even the woman who likes to be pursued needs to know how to turn the tables now and then. By following some of the steps that Slim used with Morgan, you'll gain confidence and the kind of take-charge attitude that many men love. Who knows, you may even catch your man just like Bacall caught Bogie.

The Aggressive Kiss

TAUNTING Slim begins by taunting the man she likes. You, too, can use verbal pyrotechnics if a guy isn't giving you the attention—and the kisses—you deserve.

INVADING Being the aggressor means taking risks. Slim actually sits on Morgan's lap to get things moving. Her hand on his chest, her face close to his, she hopes he'll make a move, but she's not going to spend all day waiting.

CLOSING Closing the gap between them, she looks him directly in the eyes and gets close enough for him to feel the heat from her face on his. If you want a shy guy to kiss you, you may need to use the same aggressive tactics.

MOVING Moving in for the kill, Slim initiates the kiss. Morgan doesn't even lean forward to help her. Some men are too shy, too inexperienced, or simply too into themselves to make a first move. Sometimes a girl needs to know how to do it herself!

The Tryst Kiss

LOVERS ARE ALWAYS making plans to meet, and a romantic way to seal the promise to get together at a certain place and time is with a tryst kiss, so called because it's a subtle reminder to your partner that there's more of that in store when you meet again. The most famous tryst kiss in movie history undoubtedly occurs near the end of *An Affair to Remember* (1957) between Nickie (Cary Grant) and Terry (Deborah Kerr).

The two have met on a cruise and enjoyed a wonderful shipboard romance, and when they arrive at their destination port of New York City they make plans to meet again. The only problem is that they haven't specified a place. Nickie notices the Empire State Building in the background and suggests they meet there. Of course he has no idea what fate holds in store for them or how Terry will accidentally be prevented from keeping the date, so they blithely seal the pact with a kiss. The tryst kiss, as done here by Nickie and Terry, is important for three reasons. First, it seals the promise to meet at the designated time and place.

Second, it states that you currently love each other. Third, it suggests that there's more in the way of romantic kisses when you get together again. As such, it's a special form of the goodbye kiss, one in which you promise to meet a lover at a specified time and place in the future. Because the tryst kiss differs from the normal goodbye kiss in that you have selected a specific time and place to meet, the kiss offers the opportunity to enjoy a more meaningful and emotional connection before breaking apart. Indeed, the kiss allows Nickie to communicate some of his romantic zeal in a promissory manner, wordlessly telling Terry that he loves her and that he plans to bring an identical passion to the meeting place they've selected. He's saying in effect, "This is what awaits you when we meet."

As he breaks off the kiss, Nickie reminds Terry that they'll both be there at the designated time and place, the 102nd floor of the Empire State Building. This reminder serves a dual purpose: It reinforces the meeting place and time and it also whets the appetite of the partners for that rendezvous. In this film Terry never made it to the meeting, but with the advent of cell phones, you can usually avoid such problems. Just remember to use a kiss to seal the promise to meet and you can be sure that your partner will be thinking of you until you see each other again.

The Tryst Kiss

MAKING THE DATE Nickie and Terry have made a date to meet atop the Empire State Building. When you make a date like this it's a good idea to exchange cell phone numbers, just in case something comes up. Of course, in those days they didn't have cell phones. . . .

SEALING THE PROMISE WITH A KISS Even today, when we *do* have cell phones, it's a good idea to seal your promise to meet with a tryst kiss. The kiss is romantic because it suggests that you'll be thinking of your partner until you meet again.

REMINDING YOUR PARTNER After breaking off the tryst kiss, Nickie assures Terry that they'll both be there at the meeting they've planned. Little does he know, of course, that she will not. A tryst kiss can keep you in the heart and mind of your partner until you *do* see each other again.

The
Secret Kiss

WHEN YOU AND your partner share a special secret, a kiss can help you keep it to yourselves. The method of giving a secret kiss is illustrated in *Cinderella Man* (2005) when World Heavyweight Boxing Champion Jim Braddock (Russell Crowe) kisses his wife, Mae (Renée Zellweger). The scene in question involves Jim trying to persuade Mae to let him get back into the ring.

At first the secret is all Jim's; his wife has no idea he wants to fight again. When he tells her his plans, she's not too happy because, like most wives of fighters, she fears that he may get hurt in the ring. At first he's reassuring her that he'll be fine: he picks her up in his arms, makes eye contact, and talks to her softly. Their interaction has certain level of warmth not found in most kisses because they're talking and having an emotional discussion prior to their lip contact. When sharing a secret, a dream, or a confidential plan of action, it's a good idea to talk it over in hushed tones, like Jim and Mae are doing here. When Jim finally kisses her, the kiss is sweet and innocent, but it's also full of meaning because he's trying to convince her that he'll be fine and that she has nothing to worry about. Mae takes the kiss like a loving spouse, but she's still somewhat reticent. Clearly she has her doubts about Jim's plans. Yet a secret shared over a kiss is one that brings the two much closer together than words alone could.

After their initial kiss they break apart, with Jim still holding Mae, and they continue their conversation. Mae was dead set against the idea at the outset, but she quiets down and at least *listens* to Jim's point of view now, even though she doesn't come right out and agree with it. The kiss continues for a while longer, after which Jim lets Mae down to her feet. She gives him a searching look, as if still wondering about his decision. Maybe she's not resigned to the plan he has in mind, but now she's at least privy to the secret information. When you share a secret it can bring you closer, especially when it's sealed with a kiss.

The Secret Kiss

SHARING Jim shares his secret dream with Mae, telling her he wants to get back into the ring. When sharing a secret like this, one that involves the two of you intimately, it helps to discuss the matter at close quarters.

KISSING The kisses you give when talking over a secret are intended to bring you closer so that you can understand your partner's point of view.

TALKING Interrupting a secret kiss with more talking is a normal procedure. Jim has to get in a few more words because his news and his plan are so controversial. The fact that he's talking in the context of a kiss makes their conversation much more meaningful and important.

MORE KISSING A few more kisses are always in order when you're this close, and Jim doesn't hesitate to kiss Mae as he continues to share his plans. Mae puts her arms around his neck and leans forward slightly so that she's fully present in the secret kiss.

Playful Kissing

A PLAYFUL SPIRIT and kissing go together perfectly, and most good kisses have some element of playfulness about them. To examine this all-important aspect of kissing, let's turn to a scene in which the woman gets the man to adopt her playful attitude: the kiss between Natalie (Maria Bello) and Bernie (William H. Macy) in *The Cooler* (2003).

Their kiss begins with Natalie inviting Bernie to sit beside her. Her expression is one of uninhibited joy, her invitation one he can't resist, and her manner absolutely playful. Getting your partner to your side can sometimes be a chore, but when you have the same upbeat attitude as Natalie, the task can be accomplished much more easily, and the two of you can take the next step toward the kiss. Bernie sits beside her and before he knows what's happening she clamps her open palm on his face to surprise him, to make him smile, and to show him that she's not going to be discussing anything serious. She tells him to relax, and he *does* smile, trying to get into the same frame of mind as Natalie. If your partner isn't in the right playful mood, it may become necessary for you to lighten that mood with some silly antics like Natalie uses here. Her move was spontaneous and spur-of-the-moment, and it had just the right amount of impulsive craziness to do the trick. A few seconds later Bernie is indeed smiling as he starts to come over to Natalie's way of thinking. Finally *he's* getting playful too.

When Natalie loosens his tie, Bernie has no choice but to realize that she's winning him over to her way of thinking. At this point he's playfully following along while Natalie takes the kiss in the direction she prefers. This actually allows Bernie to relax and enjoy the kiss. Natalie, meanwhile, is carefully but nonchalantly monitoring his reactions, which may be a necessary step when trying to get a straitlaced partner to play along. After she loosens his tie she wraps one hand around his neck and kisses him passionately but playfully on the mouth, using some tongue for the initial kisses. This is a seductive kiss, but it's also a playful one, which invites Bernie to have some fun and lighten up himself.

Playful kissing works best when both parties are thinking alike, but in this scene Natalie had the playful attitude, especially at the outset. She did everything she could to communicate this to her partner, and little by little she won him over. By the time she kissed Bernie, he was getting into the spirit of things and was ready to play along. If your kisses aren't playful enough, add a dash of fun and frivolity into your next kissing session, and you and your partner will surely enjoy the experience even more.

Playful Kissing

IMPULSIVE MOVES Notice that Natalie's impulsive move is quite unusual, putting her hand on his face with her fingers spread. It doesn't matter *what* you do at this point, the key is to do something out of the ordinary to get your partner smiling and relaxing.

GETTING RELAXED Going one step further, Natalie loosens Bernie's tie, suggesting that she's in the mood for a playful kiss. If you've judged your partner well, this playful attitude will produce a smile, as it does with Bernie.

WARMING UP Natalie is powerfully suggesting that Bernie should adopt her playful attitude. Her hand around his neck is intended to keep him put while she kisses him, but it also shows that she's ready to play.

FEELING PLAYFUL When both parties feel playful, kissing can be much more enjoyable. Finally, Natalie sits on Bernie's lap, inviting him to join in her playful antics. Sometimes it takes quite a bit of work to get your partner to think playfully, but Natalie's persistence succeeds in the end.

Confusing Kisses

NOT ALL KISSES ARE CLEAR and understandable; indeed, sometimes a kiss can be full of confusion and ambivalence. Such a kiss appears in *Cruel Intentions* (1999) between Sebastian (Ryan Phillippe) and his friend Annette (Reese Witherspoon).

The scene begins with Annette sitting alone in the park on a blanket. Sebastian approaches and greets her playfully, speaking in French and receiving a reply in French. At this point they're just showing off what they've learned in their high school French class. As they continue the mock civility, Sebastian leans down and gives Annette a European-style greeting kiss, in which two people kiss the air to the side of the cheek. A greeting kiss like this signals that the two are merely friends or acquaintances, not intimate lovers. But then in the next moment he escalates the greeting kiss and kisses her in a more romantic way on her cheek, actually touching her with his lips. This is no longer a simple greeting kiss. Sebastian has moved into the realm of romance. His opening kiss stirs something in Annette's heart, and before she even knows what she's doing she finds herself kissing him back. But her reply isn't a simple lip kiss, it's a full-fledged open-mouth kiss. The two have moved from a noncommittal greeting kiss—in effect an air kiss—to a cheek kiss, to an open-mouth kiss on the lips. This is seriously confusing the issue, and at this point neither of them knows where the relationship stands. In fact Annette is so confused—she likes Sebastian but wants to maintain her composure and *not* get involved with anyone she doesn't love—that she actually pushes him away. The ensuing dialogue makes clear that she can't control her feelings when she's with him and she thinks it prudent to stop kissing him for good.

When kisses cross the boundary from friendly greeting kisses to more intimate lip and tongue kisses common between lovers, feelings and intentions can become confused and difficult to define. There's no question that Sebastian and Annette both enjoyed the kiss while it was happening, but Annette has made it clear that she feels ambivalent. Because she has mixed feelings, she doesn't know whether she wants to kiss or to stop kissing. Such mixed feelings are not uncommon at the outset or at the conclusion of a relationship. The best kissing advice is to acknowledge your mixed feelings and decide whether this is truly someone you want to kiss because a kiss like this one—on the lips and with mouths open—almost always signals that a relationship has become more than casual.

Confusing Kisses

 **GREETING KISS** Sebastian gives Annette a greeting kiss, which sets the stage for the confusion that follows. When you start out like this you're saying you respect the other person as a friend, not as a lover.

 **AIR KISS** An air kiss is done to the side of the face and doesn't involve lip contact. Notice that Sebastian's lips are not in contact with Annette at this point. The kiss is still platonic or friendly.

 **CHEEK KISS** When Sebastian lets his lips touch Annette's cheek in a lingering fashion he confuses the issue. A brief cheek kiss in greeting is still platonic, but a lingering cheek kiss like this, especially one so close to the lips, is much more than friendly.

 **LIP KISS** Confusing the issue even further is the fact that Annette gives back an open-mouth kiss. Clearly these two have mixed feelings. On the one hand Annette wants to be just friends, but on the other hand she admits to having strong feelings for Sebastian. The result is a confused kiss.

The Vacuum Kiss

NO MOVIE ILLUSTRATES the vacuum kiss better than *Coneheads* (1993), a comedy that tells the story of a family from another planet living on Earth disguised as humans. In one scene Ronnie (Chris Farley) drives his date home and then attempts to kiss her. But when he kisses Connie Conehead (Michelle Burke) he gets the surprise of his life—a vacuum kiss. The scene is funny and also nicely illustrates the essential aspects of the vacuum kiss.

The game begins when Ronnie tries to teach his girlfriend how to kiss. He tells her that kissing is easy. "All you do is lean forward and kiss, like this." Then he puckers up and leans toward Connie in the front seat of his car. His girlfriend takes the gum out of her mouth. This is a quiet prelude to the kiss and also a good idea because gum or candy can get suctioned during this kiss. Connie then puckers up just like Ronnie, which is another good idea before a vacuum kiss because it enables the kissers to get a good seal all around the mouth, preventing any air leaks which could diminish the full effect of the vacuum.

Finally Connie leans forward and presses her lips to Ronnie's. A certain amount of mutual pressure is needed so that the lips don't break apart during the inhalation and exhalation part of the kiss. Notice that Ronnie puts his hand around Connie's neck, drawing her to him and ensuring that they'll have enough pressure on their lips to produce a good lip seal.

The kiss develops from a closed-mouth kiss to an open-mouth kiss when both Ronnie and Connie open their mouths slightly, but unlike most open-mouth kisses the vacuum kiss involves no tongue. Use of the tongue would block the airflow and prevent a vacuum kiss from occurring. Once the lips are sealed and the mouths opened slightly, vacuuming can begin. In this case the girl begins by sucking the air out of Ronnie's mouth. You can see his eyes almost pop out of his head at this point.

In order for the vacuum kiss to work successfully, when the girl *in*hales the boy should simultaneously *ex*hale. This may leave the participants a little breathless at the conclusion of the kiss, and Ronnie breaks off from his first vacuum kiss looking cross-eyed and out of breath. Such a momentary reaction is normal and indicates that you've done the kiss correctly.

Any vacuum kiss can be prolonged by having one partner alternately inhale and then exhale while the other partner does just the opposite. This allows air to travel freely back and forth in what is popularly referred to as a double vacuum kiss. Since most people have never tried a vacuum kiss, it's a great way to surprise and tease your partner.

The Vacuum Kiss

VACUUMING Even before making lip contact, Connie has her lips puckered in an open position. What she has on her mind, apparently, is jumping right to the vacuum kiss. Once she makes lip contact, she'll begin to inhale forcefully.

INHALING As Connie inhales she sucks the air out of Ronnie's mouth. This process may take several seconds and, of course, requires Ronnie to open his lips slightly to let the air rush into Connie's mouth and lungs.

EXHALING It takes two to vacuum. As Connie opens wide (without breaking lip contact) and inhales, Ronnie is forced to exhale directly into her mouth.

RECOVERING Slightly cross-eyed and light-headed, it takes Ronnie a few moments to recover. Any good vacuum kiss will leave you feeling pleasantly breathless and excited.

The Ice-Cream Kiss

WHEN YOU'RE IN LOVE it certainly helps to have a sense of humor, and one of the most humorous kisses you can try is the ice-cream kiss. This kiss is sure to bring out the child in anyone. A high-energy example of this kiss appears in *The Notebook* (2004) as two young lovers are walking along a suburban street on a beautiful afternoon.

The scene opens with Noah (Ryan Gosling) and Allie (Rachel McAdams) having just come out of an ice-cream parlor. There are smiles on their faces and even the people in the background seem to be enjoying the nice weather—everything looks peaceful and idyllic. Noah and Allie have been dating for a while and both seem to be in a fun and relaxed frame of mind as they stroll down the street. Allie has an ice-cream cone in her hand and Noah is looking at her with a loving expression. Then suddenly and without any warning whatsoever, she grins and shoves her ice-cream cone right into her boyfriend's face. Nothing could have prepared him for *this*. Understandably, Noah is astonished. Reeling in confusion, he falls against one of the shops along the street, his back to the storefront.

But Allie is just playing with him, and as Noah falls back in surprise she grabs him and wraps one hand around his head and laughingly kisses him, slurping ice cream off his lips and face. All the while she's smiling and giggling and Noah is trying to get his bearings. There's so much ice cream on his face that he can hardly see. Through his grimacing he finds time to catch a breath and mimic his playful girlfriend by being a good sport and kissing her back. Meanwhile, she's kissing him with a classic lip-o-suction kiss, first on the upper lip, then on the lower lip. With each kiss she slurps more ice cream off her discombobulated boyfriend.

In response to this licking by Allie, Noah finally fights back by rubbing his face playfully against hers, getting some ice cream on her too. And so they continue to play, licking and kissing ice cream off each other, paying no heed to people who pass by, enjoying their own little game. There's no question that they're having fun because after Noah gets over his shock he smiles and laughs while Allie kisses him. And by the end of the kiss she's laughing so hysterically that she can hardly stand.

The Ice-Cream Kiss

ICE CREAM IS FOR SHARING . . . Allie and Noah are on a date but only *one* of them has an ice-cream cone. Noah is looking at the ice cream as if he wants some. She's not going to keep it all to herself, is she?

A SPECIAL KIND OF SHARING In a moment of impulsive fun, Allie smashes her ice-cream cone right into her boyfriend's face, careful to push it up into his nose and all over his mouth and chin. What can she be thinking!

KISSING THE ICE CREAM OFF Allie makes it clear that she's just goofing around as she kisses the ice cream off him, one delicious spot at a time. This is a messy job but she gets right into it without hesitation.

GETTING INTO THE ACT Allie is making amends by cleaning Noah off, but he's not really offended. He's enjoying it, and he's getting into the act too, kissing Allie back and licking the ice cream off her face and lips. This is a kiss that both can savor equally.

The
Victory Kiss

CELEBRATING A VICTORY with a kiss is often a good idea, especially when the person you're celebrating with is your boyfriend or girlfriend. Victory kisses can be given upon buying a new house, winning a football game, or to mark any special occasion when someone has achieved something substantial. A good example of a victory kiss between a boyfriend and girlfriend appears near the end of *Pleasantville* (1998) when Bud (Tobey Maguire) kisses his girlfriend Margaret (Marley Shelton). Their kiss occurs outside on a sunny day in Pleasantville, a fictitious town where things are always pleasant. This victory kiss is heartwarming and illustrates nicely how to kiss in such a situation.

Margaret runs up to Bud through a crowd of people outside the courtroom. This is how many victory kisses start—with one person running up to another in a crowded area—because during a victory there are often other people present and well-wishers may be eager to say nice things even if they have to fight their way through a crowd to get to the victorious person. Of course a victory kiss can be done in private, but in this case the victory is celebrated with a kiss in front of many onlookers, and that doesn't diminish its power one whit; in fact, the kiss in this situation has added poignancy because it's a statement of the affection between Bud and his new girlfriend, Margaret. She's so happy with the way Bud spoke up in court that she literally jumps into his arms, embracing him and holding him tight, her arms wrapped around his neck in an affectionate and celebratory manner. For his part, Bud holds her tenderly and turns around in joy, glad to be reunited with her in this victorious moment.

Bud then lets her down to her feet. At this point Margaret tilts her head to the side slightly, looks fondly into his eyes as if to say "Congratulations!" and then the two young people move together for the victory kiss itself. Margaret puts her hands gently and lovingly around Bud's face, caressing him and kissing him on the lips. Bud closes his eyes and kisses her back, glad to be able to celebrate this victory with the girl he loves. A victory kiss is a perfect way to celebrate because victory itself can be stressful, and the connection with someone you love is usually calming.

At the last moment Bud's sister interrupts and he turns to her, but interruptions during moments of celebration don't really diminish the fun; on the contrary, that's what celebrations are for— sharing the joy of victory and being sociable with those who care for you and who want to wish you well. The victory kiss is a moment of joy shared between two people, and when they love each other that moment will seem to last forever, as it does in this victory kiss in *Pleasantville*.

The Victory Kiss

GETTING TO THE VICTOR Margaret has to rush through a crowd to get to Bud. Notice that she smiles when she sees him. A victory kiss is just as thrilling for the giver as it is for the recipient. The very fact that this kiss is often done in a crowd can actually add to the fun and excitement of the moment.

JUMPING WITH JOY Margaret doesn't care if people see her jump into Bud's arms, and a victory celebration is a legitimate time for doing something exuberant and joyously unrestrained like this.

VICTORY KISS The victory kiss momentarily isolates the two kissers in a world of their own amid the hustle and bustle of the crowds that are standing nearby. As their lips get closer for a kiss, their world contracts until it holds just the two of them and their joy at being together.

CARESSING GENTLY Margaret gently holds Bud's face as she kisses him, celebrating his victory with a very special kiss. The moment is at once celebratory and romantic. Her love and affection are just what the victor needs at this moment to make him feel that he's done the right thing.

The Rebellious Kiss

THE ESSENCE OF LOVE is union and togetherness, but in order to achieve that state of supreme happiness you must sometimes rebel against various outside forces that may be working to keep you apart: society, friends, or even family. At the moment when you realize that you must fight for love, the spirit of rebellion is born and the possibility exists for one of the most exciting kisses of all, the rebellious kiss. A perfect example of this kiss appears in *The House of the Spirits* (1993). Blanca (Winona Ryder) and Pedro (Antonio Banderas) kiss outside on a night when everything seems impossible for them, in a land where their love is outlawed, and at a time when revolution is in the air.

The scene opens with Blanca running to a secret rendezvous with her revolutionary boyfriend, Pedro. Blanca's parents are very conservative and they dislike the fact that their daughter is interested in this outsider. As a result she has to sneak to her meeting with him down by the river. In many ways their story involves the classic forbidden love of two young people from divergent backgrounds: she's from a wealthy aristocratic South American family, and he's a worker on her father's farm and a revolutionary. When they meet they're excited but also afraid because danger surrounds them, and if they're found together Blanca's father would not be pleased. Blanca, however, is not one to be cowed by reason or intellectual arguments when her feelings are involved, and she enthusiastically embraces Pedro, telling him that she loves him.

Hugging the impulsive Blanca to him tightly, Pedro kisses her back passionately, although his heart is filled with foreboding. Knowing much more than she does about the social climate and the situation on the farm, he senses that what they're doing is going to cause trouble in her family and, ultimately, with the desperate men leading the revolution. And yet despite these obstacles to their love, the two share a moment of togetherness and a fleeting rebellious kiss that says that their love is more important than all the social upheaval going on around them, more important, even, than the wishes of an older, more conservative generation. The rebellious kiss is full of passion, commitment, and urgency. When Blanca breaks off for a moment to gaze imploringly into Pedro's eyes, she assures him of her love, and he swears that he feels the same way. But they are not the sole masters of their fate; they are enmeshed in a situation that conspires to keep them apart. After a few words of endearment, they continue their kiss, wresting a bittersweet moment of joy from a world that seems dead set against them. When two people are pitted against the rest of the world like this, it's understandable that their kisses will take on some of the flavor of rebellion, and a very exciting and romantic flavor it is.

The Rebellious Kiss

SECRET RENDEZVOUS Blanca's secret rendezvous with her boyfriend, Pedro, is exciting precisely *because* it is secret. Sometimes young people caught up in the spirit of love decide to take chances like this, and kisses done in such situations seem to them like the most wonderful reward for all their plotting and scheming.

SURROUNDED BY DANGER In fact, Blanca and Pedro are surrounded by real danger, and this quickens their hearts and brings them even closer together. Allies against the world, they cling to each other as if that's all that matters.

REBEL AT HEART Because Pedro is a true revolutionary, he already has the requisite rebellious spirit. Blanca is going against the express wishes of her parents. Both rebels at heart, they're a perfect match.

HOPING FOR THE BEST Naturally they hope for the best, but under the circumstances that's somewhat unrealistic. Love, however, is not realistic; it's passionate, spirited, and tempestuous. When rebelliousness is added to the mix, the sparks that unite two young lovers like Blanca and Pedro are full of romance.

The
Car Kiss

KISSING IN CARS is such a part of modern culture that almost everyone has done it. But like anything else, technique can always be improved, and movie kisses can suggest helpful pointers for your next date. An instructive example of a car kiss appears in David Lynch's *Mulholland Drive* (2001) as a movie director (Justin Theroux) explains to an actor (Laura Harring) exactly how to do a car kiss for a film he's shooting.

The scene begins with Adam (the director) putting his right arm around Rita. At the same time, he brings his left hand up under her chin, giving him some control over the angle of her head and allowing him to make minor adjustments as needed before and during the kiss. Another important point to note at this stage is the body position of the couple. Because cars don't afford much room for movement, it's vital to use what room you do have to maximum effect. Adam turns his body slightly toward his partner, which is all that's really necessary to get a car kiss going.

The next step is up to Rita. If she wants to be kissed, her best option is to lean in toward Adam, as Rita does. Although many people (66 percent) like to keep their eyes closed when they kiss, Rita still has hers open. This is also a good idea for a car kiss, just to be sure that you're in the proper position. Once your lips actually connect you can close your eyes if you wish. For Adam, the second stage of the car kiss is relatively easy—all he has to do is sit there and guide Rita toward him with his hand under her chin, as he's doing here.

In the third step Rita turns her head up and opens her lips slightly for the kiss. Adam keeps his hand under her chin, gently guiding her toward him for the initial contact. Once your lips connect you can get creative; indeed, there are many different types of kisses you can enjoy in a car, including lip-o-suction, the vacuum kiss, and the French kiss. Notice that Adam isn't kneeling on the car seat and neither is Rita; in fact, they haven't turned their bodies more than fifteen or twenty degrees toward each other. The person behind the steering wheel is the one who is most limited in what he can do, but even so, not much body twisting is really needed for a front-seat kiss.

Next comes the reaction phase of the kiss, during which Rita smiles broadly at her partner. Most people occasionally giggle when kissing, but if your partner laughs, don't get insulted. She's not laughing *at* you, her reaction is a sign of pleasure. On the other hand, Adam struggles to remain deadpan in his reaction because it's considered bad form for an actor to get significant personal pleasure from a kiss, especially during rehearsal. The truth is, however, that he's hiding his real feelings for Rita. This is another important point to remember when kissing in a car, or anywhere else for that matter: One person is always more into the kiss and enjoys it more. In other words, it's unrealistic to expect two people to have identical reactions to any particular kiss. The difference in their reactions isn't significant, however, and you shouldn't read anything into the fact that you and your partner react somewhat differently.

In the final stage of the kiss, the couple is eye to eye again, their noses touching and their lips only millimeters apart. Naturally, they're getting set for another kiss. One of the pleasures of kissing in a car is that you're in a cozy intimate space and yet people can see you through the windows. It's enough to make any exhibitionist want to kiss all night.

The Car Kiss

LOOKING AT EACH OTHER Adam and Rita are regarding each other with a look that says romance. Put your hand under your girlfriend's chin, as Adam does here, guiding her to you and reassuring her as you close in for a car kiss.

LEANING CLOSE Rita makes the right move, sliding close to Adam and letting him guide her chin up slightly. Keep your eyes open until you're in position, just in case your partner shifts the angle of his jaw before contact.

RECEIVING THE KISS Adam receives the kiss without moving appreciably. Rita angles her chin up and into the kiss, taking guidance from his hand, which is still under her chin. This stage of the car kiss can be prolonged for quite some time and is, of course, the best part of the whole experience.

ANOTHER KISS Adam and Rita are getting ready to kiss again, enjoying a great romantic tradition—the car kiss. On a related note, once you start kissing you might even want to turn on the car radio to listen to your favorite songs as you kiss.

More than a Friendly Kiss

MANY LOVERS START OUT AS FRIENDS, and when their relationship moves on to another level a kiss usually marks the transition. Although friends may kiss in greeting, especially after a long absence, the kiss that signals a progression to being more than friends is a different kind of kiss altogether and often has its own special place and significance in the memories of the two people involved. A good example of this kiss occurs in *The Prince of Tides* (1991) between Tom (Nick Nolte) and psychiatrist Dr. Lowenstein (Barbra Streisand), who is caring for Tom's sister. Their kiss occurs one night after they've known each other for a number of weeks and have come to like each other as more than doctor and patient.

A kiss that marks the transition to being more than friends always has a quality of passion that makes it different from all the kisses with this person that have preceded it—if there were any—and all the kisses that follow it. The transitional kiss is the only one where the change actually occurs in the relationship, and as a result it usually begins tentatively and ends with an increase in passion and feeling. This kiss between Tom and Dr. Lowenstein follows the pattern, beginning with Tom kissing the doctor's hair as he caresses her gently. Then Dr. Lowenstein turns around and Tom kisses her softly on the mouth, signaling that this is more than a friendly kiss. The way he takes his time and lingers on her lips is the chief indication that this is a romantic kiss. After that, things get even more passionate and both kiss more fervently and lovingly than ever.

Because their relationship has been developing over the course of many meetings, both business and social, by the time they kiss they have a great understanding of each other. This understanding gives the kiss added emotional meaning and may lead them to have great expectations about their new relationship. Such expectations have both intellectual and emotional elements. On the one hand, they see a change taking place, which is something they may have expected logically, but on the other hand they're falling in love, which is something they feel emotionally and which may be disorienting and exhilarating. Perhaps these feelings are the reason why a kiss like this is often remembered for a lifetime.

Tom is rather insistent when he kisses the doctor's lips, and the doctor replies in kind, both of them very glad that their relationship has advanced to this stage. One of the keys to understanding this particular kiss is the way that Tom moves his lips across the doctor's hair, neck, and face while she leans against the wall. The passion he feels for her is expressed in his moving from place to place across her body as if he can't get enough of her love. She is receptive to his kiss as if it were the most natural thing in the world. It may mean different things to different people when a relationship has moved from simple friendship to romance and love, but the kiss that marks such a transition is always a memorable experience.

More than a Friendly Kiss

MAKING THE TRANSITION Embracing at last, Tom and Dr. Lowenstein are finally making the transition from being friends to being more than friends. Their relationship is becoming deeper, and this hug is the beginning of that transition.

KISSING THE HAIR The kiss that's more than a friendly kiss is often filled with passion, tenderness, and a sense of relief that things have finally progressed to this point. Here, Tom is immersed in these feelings and almost can't wait to kiss the doctor. He begins by kissing her hair softly in preparation for a kiss on the lips.

ACTIVE AND PASSIVE KISSING Tom takes an active role while Dr. Lowenstein is more passive here, leaning against the wall to accept his kisses. Sometimes one of the partners in such a situation can't believe what's happening, and it takes the doctor a moment to get used to the new relationship.

RESPONDING WITH PASSION The doctor quickly responds with passion. Her fervor and Tom's continued insistent kisses make this much more than a friendly kiss. A kiss like this can make an indelible impression because after it occurs things will never be the same.

The
Hard-to-Get
Kiss

IF KISSING WERE always the same it would quickly become boring and trivial, which is why it's important to vary your style and approach. One intriguing variation that's relatively easy to introduce into your kissing sessions is a game called playing hard to get. A colorful and spirited example of this technique appears in *William Shakespeare's Romeo + Juliet* (1996), directed by Baz Luhrmann. The kiss between Romeo (Leonardo DiCaprio) and Juliet (Claire Danes) occurs at the Capulet mansion during a party.

Baz Luhrmann adds an interesting twist to Romeo and Juliet's first kiss, with a flirtatious game of hard-to-get. The scene begins as the two young lovers stare into each other's eyes, drunk with infatuation, feeling all the effects of love at first sight. For the audience, understanding that background only heightens the fun of what happens next because we know how intensely they're drawn to each other. Yet as Romeo leans in for that first kiss, moving slowly but determinedly down toward Juliet's lips, she surprises him by smiling gaily and turning her head aside, playing hard to get. She teases the young man into following her as she runs away, her costume of angel's wings and his of Roman armor lending an even more romantic air to the whole proceeding. The party swirls on about them, and the two are now caught up in a dance of love that moves swiftly on to its sweet conclusion.

Having hidden away in another part of the mansion, sliding between doors and columns, Juliet awaits her new paramour. She doesn't have long to wait as her provocative behavior and teasing attitude have whetted Romeo's appetite for a kiss. Playing hard to get will often increase desire in a partner, as it does here, drawing him to you with renewed attentiveness and fervor until at last his lips seek yours. Romeo finds Juliet more receptive this time, though no less lighthearted and full of fun, and he kisses her gently, lovingly, and tenderly. The young lady returns his kiss with passion and love, the two now locked in an embrace of infatuation, heartened by their flirtation, and cheered by their playfulness. The tenor of their kiss has moved from teasing to loving, allowing them to luxuriate in the glow of a mutually affectionate embrace. Playing hard to get has its rewards, and if you relent and allow the kiss to occur quickly afterward, as Juliet does here, you'll find that the technique will work its magic for you as well.

The Hard-to-Get Kiss

LOOKING FOR LOVE Juliet, of course, falls in love with Romeo as quickly as he falls in love with her. Such is the nature of love at first sight. That doesn't mean, however, that she'll let him kiss her without playing hard to get.

TRYING TO KISS Romeo, drawn irresistibly to the object of his desire, tries to kiss Juliet at the Capulets' party. She wants to kiss him as much as he wants to kiss her, but what is her response? She smiles and pulls back, teasing him to fan the flames of his ardor.

PULLING AWAY Not content simply to pull her head back, Juliet actually turns aside and runs from Romeo, playfully of course, secure in the knowledge that the cat will chase the mouse. So sure is she that he'll follow that she smiles as she goes, knowing it's all a game. *This* is how to play hard to get.

TOGETHER AT LAST When finally she slows to a stop and allows Romeo to touch his lips to hers, the connection is that much sweeter. Romeo has no complaints with Juliet's playing hard to get; indeed, the fact that she was so feisty and flirtatious has increased his desire. For both of them this little game has had a very satisfactory conclusion.

The Distracting Kiss

A DISTRACTING KISS allows you to focus your partner's attention on the kiss itself so that you can fish for information without her noticing. This kiss is invitational in nature since it invites your partner to loosen up and kiss you back and, incidentally, to cooperate with your questioning. A perfect example of this kiss occurs in Stanley Kubrick's *Eyes Wide Shut* (1999) when Dr. Harford (Tom Cruise) kisses his wife, Alice (Nicole Kidman). Dr. Harford is trying to get Alice to reveal some information about a man she was flirting with earlier in the evening at a party.

The distracting kiss always has a double-edged quality. On the one hand it's a kiss like any other with romantic and sensual overtones, but on the other hand it's aimed at getting your partner to be friendly and open when you're seeking information, such as Dr. Harford is doing in this scene. The kiss begins with the doctor kissing Alice on the side of the face. He asks her some questions and then breaks off the kiss to look directly at her to hear her answer.

When she doesn't tell him exactly what he wants to know, he gets back to the distracting kiss, this time moving to her shoulder. While kissing his wife, he intermittently asks questions and carries on a conversation. His kiss is basically diversionary and even slightly comical when viewed in light of what he's trying to do.

Finally the doctor kisses the side of Alice's face again. This progression from one part of the body to another is typical of a distracting kiss. The kisser is trying to be sweet and loving while at the same time needling his wife for information. Kisses like this can have either of two outcomes: They can lead to an increase in kissing and a reciprocated kiss, in which case things turn more romantic, or, as in this scene, they can lead to the kissee becoming suspicious and moving away. In order to get the more romantic outcome, it's vitally important to give the kiss in such a way that you don't focus too heavily on the cross-examination process. Dr. Harford makes the mistake of pushing his conversation into sensitive areas that are upsetting to his wife, but by avoiding such topics and asking simpler questions, your results can be much more tender and loving, and you're likely to get pleasant, gentle kisses instead of a cross-examination in return.

The Distracting Kiss

KISSING THE CHEEK The doctor begins by kissing his wife's cheek, hoping she'll tell him what he wants to know. This kiss is distracting in the sense that he's hoping she'll focus on the kiss and not think too much about what he's asking.

BREAKING OFF MOMENTARILY Notice that Alice is looking away. So far, the distracting kiss isn't working properly because she's not kissing back or becoming romantic in return.

BACK TO THE SHOULDER The doctor continues his questioning while at the same time continuing to kiss Alice's shoulder. Again he hopes that his distracting kiss will put his wife in a good frame of mind and encourage her to open up about her recent flirtation.

MOVING TO THE EAR The doctor kisses Alice's ear in a last-ditch effort to distract her. But he's too late. She's already moving away from him. The key to successful distracting kisses is to do them more sweetly and with fewer questions interrupting the kiss.

PART THREE

Kissing Techniques

You need two things for a good kiss— passion and technique. What if you've got one and not the other? Disaster! All the technique in the world won't help if you've got no fire in your heart. And all the passion in the world won't do you any good if your technique is horrible. Of these two essentials, only technique can be taught. Once you have that all-important romantic connection in place, there are plenty of kissing techniques you can learn from movies. You can dramatically improve your kissing style by varying the intensity of a kiss, by kissing in various fun ways, and by learning the crucial skill of slow kissing. When watching romantic scenes, pay particular attention to how good actors receive a kiss and how they get back into a kiss after an interruption. Sophisticated lovers are always eager to learn new things and improve their technique. The films in Part III will help you pick up and perfect a few of the more essential kissing skills. And you don't have to admit to anyone that you learned it from a movie.

How to Receive a Kiss

IN KISSING, someone is always more active, someone more receptive. This give and take is one of the things that makes kissing fun, and the interplay can go back and forth with one being the more active at the outset and then the other taking over and being more active later, so that the initiative passes from person to person a number of times during the course of a few minutes. But sometimes—because of preference, inclination, or simply because of your relationship to the kisser—you'll find yourself merely the recipient of a kiss. In such circumstances, what attitude should you adopt? The answer to this question illuminates a charming scene at the beginning of *Notting Hill* (1999).

Anna (Julia Roberts) is a famous movie star, and William (Hugh Grant) is the unassuming English bookshop clerk who becomes infatuated with her. Their kiss occurs in his apartment, and it nicely illustrates how to receive a kiss.

The setup is simple enough: William has bumped into a famous actress twice in one day and has inadvertently spilled orange juice on her and then allowed her to change clothes in his apartment. In leaving she gives him a kiss. The sequence in question begins in the hallway behind his door as Anna is saying goodbye. He, of course, is in awe of her since she's the most famous film star in the world. He can hardly believe she's in his apartment. This is exactly how many people feel at the outset of a relationship when they're with the one they love—they're in awe of their potential new partner, especially if they don't think a kiss could really happen. They also dream of that kiss and hope for it. Which is precisely how William feels as he says goodbye to Anna. Then something happens and Anna surprises even herself when she leans forward to give William a goodbye kiss.

William's receptiveness is the key to the scene. He stands there, not leaning forward more than a few millimeters. Meanwhile, Anna does all the work, leaning forward, reaching out to place one hand behind his head in a gentle caress, pressing her lips to his. William receives the kiss as if it were manna from heaven. The kiss actually surprises him, and he's almost in a state of shock. He had used the word *surreal* to describe the situation only moments before, and this kiss does have a surreal quality, as if it were happening to someone else, not to him. When receiving the kiss from Anna, he's very quiet and allows her to make all the moves, which is the perfect approach to take in certain situations.

When Anna leaves, William is left stunned, marveling at his good luck. This is how to receive a kiss with humility and an open heart, ready at all times to listen to how your partner is kissing you. When one adopts this receptive attitude, even the most mundane kiss can blossom, as it does in *Notting Hill,* into true love.

How to Receive a Kiss

UNEXPECTED Sometimes a kiss is unexpected, as here when Anna returns to say goodbye to a handsome bookshop clerk. She's a famous and beautiful movie star, and *she's* the one who initiates the goodbye kiss—a kiss that leads to an unexpected romantic relationship.

STANDING STILL William would love to kiss her—what man wouldn't—but he stands still and lets *her* do all the approaching. This is receptivity at its best.

RECEIVING LIP CONTACT Sometimes receiving a kiss is more fun than giving a kiss, and certainly for William receiving this kiss on the lips is an exquisitely romantic experience. Notice that he lets her put her arm around his back; he doesn't do any reaching out himself.

WAITING AND PATIENCE William also exhibits masterful technique here, simply closing his eyes and waiting for Anna to terminate the kiss when she wishes. Sometimes doing nothing is the best thing of all. Who ever said waiting can't be fun?

Where Do the Noses Go?

MANY YOUNG PEOPLE worry about bumping noses when they kiss. If this happens, it's best to just laugh it off and continue kissing. But experienced kissers—and those who are lucky for their first few kisses—turn their head before touching lips so that they avoid this problem. A good example of how to turn your head while kissing appears in *All I Want* (2002) in a kiss between Lisa (Mandy Moore) and Jones (Elijah Wood).

The scene opens with Lisa looking expectantly at Jones. During this early stage, though, it's too soon to know which way the noses will turn. Before long they get close enough to make that crucial determination: Should I turn right, or should I turn left? Dr. Onur Güntürkün, a German psychologist, recently published research in *Nature* showing that most people turn their head to the right for a kiss, so it's a safe bet that both Lisa and Jones will turn slightly to the right, and this is exactly what happens. The basic first kiss, the greeting kiss, the good-night kiss—all these standard kisses are usually accomplished with the boy and girl turning their head to the right during the kiss. In this way, the tips of the noses pass each other and don't bump, making the transition into the kiss smooth and natural.

But that isn't the end of the story—not by a long shot. Any kissing session that continues for a few minutes can benefit from the technique used in this kissing scene where the young kissers turn their heads from side to side a number of times while making out. Eventually Lisa has turned her head to the left to get a different angle for her kiss, and this position allows her to kiss Jones on the other side of his face. Finally, they both turn their noses to the right again, even tilting their heads slightly more to facilitate their kiss. By doing a kiss like this, tilting your head from side to side, you'll ensure that your partner doesn't bump noses with you, and you'll also be sure to have a more enjoyable and complete kissing experience.

Where Do the Noses Go?

MAKING EYE CONTACT Lisa looks at Jones and builds romantic tension before the kiss. As the more experienced kisser, she knows enough to tilt her head before making lip contact, but which way will he tilt *his* head? That's the all-important question.

MAKING A DECISION When they're this close, it's time to decide which way to tilt the head. The decision is usually made in a fraction of a second, and when in doubt it's probably best to turn right.

TURNING RIGHT Lisa and Jones follow the trend, turning their heads to the right for their first kiss. Because they both turned right, their noses don't bump.

TURNING LEFT A very sophisticated thing to do while kissing is to lean back and turn your head to the other side, as Lisa has done here, allowing her to move in for a second kiss with her nose turned to the left. This kind of switching back and forth adds pleasant variety to kissing.

The Greeting Kiss

MILOS FORMAN'S *Loves of a Blonde* (1965) is a film classic about a young Czech girl, Andula (Hana Brejchová), who falls in love with a cute boy, Milda (Vladimír Pucholt). The story follows their initial meeting and shows how two people can fall in love and yet have different expectations about the relationship. By the end of the film it turns out that he's not as interested in her as she had expected. At one point she goes looking for him and arrives at his house late at night. His parents are surprised when she turns up unannounced. When he arrives home and sees Andula sitting alone wrapped in a sheet taking a nap, he goes up to greet her with a kiss. Despite the fact that their relationship is not yet very deep, the greeting kiss in *Loves of a Blonde* is a wonderful example of this important technique.

Spontaneity is the key to a successful greeting kiss because you never know where you're going to meet your partner and you never know exactly how she'll be standing or sitting when you come upon her. So you have to be alert to change your technique to fit the circumstances. In this film, the boy finds Andula sitting wrapped in a sheet because she was sleeping just before he arrived— a rather unusual situation. The first thing Milda does is sit beside her. The next thing he does is get close enough for a kiss. He puts his left arm gently around her neck, drawing her to him. By gently guiding your partner close to you, you ensure that she's receptive to a kiss and close enough to receive it. Finally, he kisses her hair. You can give a greeting kiss to your partner's hair, cheek, or lips. The point is to get close, put yourself on the same plane as your partner, guide her to you and then give her a hello kiss. By following the steps illustrated in *Loves of a Blonde,* you'll ensure that all your greeting kisses are loving gestures. And when you greet a lover this way, she'll feel you've got plenty more love to give.

The Greeting Kiss

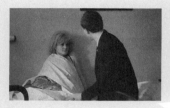

GETTING CLOSE ENOUGH TO KISS At first he gets close enough to greet her with a smile and friendly words. This is only the first step. At this initial stage of a greeting kiss you're calculating how better to move to the next step, which is touching with the hand.

BRINGING HER TOWARD YOU The use of the hand in a greeting kiss serves two purposes. First, it calms your partner with a loving touch. Second, it draws her into the exact position needed for you to give the greeting kiss.

KISSING TO SAY HELLO The conclusion of a greeting kiss is the actual touching of your lips to your lover's face or hair. In *Loves of a Blonde,* Milda gives tender greeting kisses to the back of Andula's head. You may wish to practice a new greeting kiss every time you say hello to your partner.

The Almost Kiss

NO LOVE LIFE can be considered complete without the experience of the almost kiss, a kiss that *almost* happens but then, at the final moment, doesn't. The most magical of almost kisses occurs in Federico Fellini's *La Dolce vita* (1960). Marcello (Marcello Mastroianni) is a playboy who lives a life of pleasure, seeking parties, women, and wine. Sylvia (Anita Ekberg) is a beautiful movie star who comes to Rome and spends a few days with him. During one unforgettable sequence she takes a late-night bath in the Trevi Fountain. You may have experienced an almost kiss yourself, and if so you can learn from Marcello's. The first thing that will happen is you'll be bewitched, bemused, enthralled, and otherwise taken beyond your senses because of your infatuation. Fellini's scene presents the kiss from Marcello's point of view, but women are just as susceptible to romantic infatuation as men are, and the same thing could happen to a woman who becomes enamored of a man and follows him hoping for love. Remember that an almost kiss is often the beginning of a wonderful romance because it can be the precursor to real kisses.

Marcello sits watching her as if spellbound. He can't believe what she's doing, but when she calls to him like the Sirens, he can't resist. Keep in mind that when you follow your heart's desire into the fountain, like Marcello, you may be chasing a dream. On the other hand, this may simply be chapter one in the romantic story of your life. At least that's what Marcello thinks as he follows her and almost touches her. If you're not sure whether someone reciprocates your feelings, perhaps it's better to use discretion, like Marcello does here. He almost touches her but ultimately doesn't. Neither pulls away, but after a while, as Marcello stands infatuated before Sylvia in the fountain, she reaches down and sprinkles a few drops of water on him. When you get lost in romantic fantasies, listen to your heart and decide whether you're only dreaming or whether this is reality. At this point he's nearly worshipping her. If you tend to worship the man or woman of your dreams, you may be living in a fantasy.

Finally Marcello whispers her name and gets so close to her that a kiss is just millimeters away. They look into each other's eyes, and the fantasy reaches its peak. After that the moment is over and they go their separate ways, Marcello returning to reality. If the same thing happens to you—and what lover hasn't experienced this kind of all-consuming infatuation!—you must recognize that an almost kiss is nothing to be ashamed of. Learn from it, and, if you can, pursue your dream.

The Almost Kiss

SO LOVELY Anita Ekberg in the Trevi Fountain scene symbolizes all that is desirable, all that is lovely, all that we wish for in a lover. When you see this vision in your life, you'll know that magic is happening.

SO LONELY Marcello is like Ulysses, called by the Sirens. He can't resist. It's always this way at the outset of an almost kiss, with one person drawn to another with the force of love.

SO ENCHANTED The capacity to fall in love is a universal human phenomenon. Of course, it's always better when the love is mutual. But even if it's not, you can learn from the experience.

SO FAR So close and yet so far. The kiss doesn't happen, although it almost does. An almost kiss can leave you tantalized and wanting another date. Sometimes that's a good feeling and the kiss will occur next time you meet. Sometimes, however, as in this film, nothing more ever happens.

Kissing at Curbside

AN INCREASINGLY IMPORTANT technique for the cosmopolitan romantic involves kissing at curbside. A fine example of the proper technique occurs in *Bounce* (2000). The scene is set at the side of the curb on a busy street where Buddy (Ben Affleck) and Abby (Gwyneth Paltrow) are talking. The hustle and bustle of sidewalk traffic often makes the center of the sidewalk a poor choice for a kiss, especially one that you want to have romantic significance. A better location would be closer to the curb, a spot which substantially reduces the likelihood of interruptions. Buddy and Abby walk to curbside as if they sense that they'd like to connect with a kiss. Not only are they out of the way of traffic, but they have also secured the help of a nearby tree that will provide at least a modicum of privacy for their public kiss. Notice that they're positioned so that Abby's back is to the street and Buddy's back is to passersby on the sidewalk. This setup is ideal, allowing one to monitor the street while the other watches the sidewalk. Being aware of your surroundings is an essential city survival skill, and in this position they can be sure that when they kiss they will have chosen an opportune moment, that is, a time when no crowds of pedestrians or noisy vehicles are headed their way.

Buddy signals that a kiss is imminent by touching Abby gently on the side of her face, drawing her to him and moving closer himself. At this juncture, the cars whizzing by in the background aren't a serious distraction. These two have in effect carved out a space for themselves in the middle of the city, and when they finally kiss they are, at least momentarily, in another world. Their curbside kiss is executed very tenderly, with Buddy keeping his hand gently on the side of Abby's face, guiding the kiss to its natural conclusion. Observe your surroundings and choose your romantic setting as carefully as these two and you'll enjoy your curbside kisses all the more.

Kissing at Curbside

ON THE SIDEWALK Before kissing on a crowded city sidewalk, it helps to survey the area with at least a glance to make sure the time and location are appropriate. Here, Buddy and Abby are too close to the center of the traffic path for comfort.

AT CURBSIDE Now that they've moved to a more convenient location, they've also put a tree between themselves and oncoming traffic. Not only are they safer, but they have some privacy too.

GUIDING THE KISS Buddy gently places his hand on the side of Abby's face, guiding the kiss. His light touch also provides a sense of shelter that can be calming when enjoying a curbside kiss.

LOST IN A KISS Naturally it would be fool-hardy to forget your surroundings *entirely* when kissing at curbside, but becoming lost for a few moments can be a lot of fun!

Interrupted Kisses

NOT ALL KISSES OCCUR in a totally peaceful environment. Sometimes you'll be rudely interrupted right in the middle of an affectionate embrace. One of the most visually stunning interruptions of a kiss in film history is the moment when the ship hits the iceberg in *Titanic* (1997). Jack (Leonardo DiCaprio) is on deck kissing Rose (Kate Winslet) at the time, and their reaction is a good example of how to deal with an unpleasant interruption.

Rose is looking into Jack's starlit eyes at the front of the ship. Neither of them has any idea that an iceberg lies ahead. Not surprisingly, they blithely commence kissing, oblivious of all that is around them. Before long Jack and Rose are totally into the kiss and couldn't care less what's happening with the ship. Of course the interruption here is more significant than most, but their problem is the same: When a kiss is interrupted, what's the best thing to do?

Jack and Rose have heard the crash of the ship and have felt the shudders that wracked its hull when it smashed into the iceberg, and they break off their kiss to stare in wonder at the devastation all around them—large chunks of ice splintering off from the main berg and careening down onto the deck, men running in panic, chaos everywhere. Their reaction, natural and unpremeditated, is one of shock and dismay. But it isn't long before they're inside the ship and kissing again. The fact that they're kissing so soon afterward is movie magic more than anything realistic, but the theme of this sequence is clear: Interruptions are no reason to stop kissing for long. When you have to break to answer the phone or take care of some other little emergency, the best way to recover is the way it's done in *Titanic*—get right back to kissing as soon as you can.

KISSING ON DECK Before being interrupted, Jack and Rose are kissing on deck. The night air is romantic and they're willing to enjoy a few moments of pleasure without another care in the world.

INTO ANOTHER WORLD The key to great kissing is to lose yourself in the moment, forget your worries, and let the enjoyment of lip contact take you to another time and place. Jack and Rose appear to have adopted this philosophy.

INTERRUPTED BY AN ICEBERG When the *Titanic* crashes into an iceberg, they're smart enough to break off their kiss—at least momentarily. It's a wise kisser who tends to big emergencies. But keep in mind the final piece of advice that *Titanic* offers. . . .

BACK ON TRACK As soon as possible, Jack and Rose are back together kissing again. The lesson from this scene is quite simple but very inspiring. Don't let anything—even a sinking ship—interrupt you for long. Get back to kissing as soon as you can.

Breaking off a Kiss

ALL GOOD THINGS must come to an end, including kisses, and beginning and experienced kissers alike must decide how and when to break off a kiss. The technique is not as easy as it might appear, especially for those who have little or no experience. A good example of how to break off a kiss occurs in *Bed of Roses* (1996).

The first kiss between Lewis (Christian Slater) and Lisa (Mary Stuart Masterson) occurs on a rooftop, and although the experience is pleasant, Lisa eventually feels the need to end the kiss. Her first instinct is to simply stop kissing. In fact, that's the easiest way to end a kiss: Simply cease all kissing activity, even though you don't necessarily pull back or step away from your partner. Once Lisa stops kissing, the burden, of course, falls on Lewis either to continue kissing or to follow her lead and stop as well. But when Lisa stops, Lewis doesn't immediately get the hint, so Lisa pulls back a little. This is another good way to stop a kiss, although even pulling back doesn't guarantee that your partner will realize that you wish to stop—sometimes he'll think that you're playing hard to get and he'll continue kissing. Indeed, when Lisa pulls back, Lewis continues kissing, gently nibbling on her lower lip. As should be clear from what has transpired thus far, breaking off a kiss can be trickier than it seems.

The third thing Lisa does to end the kiss is lean her forehead against Lewis's and angle her mouth away from his ever so slightly, but enough to prevent lip contact, which further signals that she's ready to quit kissing, at least for now. Finally it becomes clear to Lewis that Lisa is really done with this kissing encounter. Sometimes feelings get hurt when one partner terminates what the other thought was a great kiss, and in this exchange Lewis looks a little disappointed and baffled by Lisa's move.

Almost as a consolation prize, Lisa rubs her nose gently against Lewis's nose, as if to say: "I'm not trying to be unkind, I *do* like you!" She also makes eye contact with him, again in an almost re-assuring way. The message is that although she wants to stop the kiss, she's not trying to stop the relationship. Mixed messages can be sent when words aren't used, so this elaborate dance of the lips, forehead, nose, and eyes is one of the best ways to signal that you wish to end a kiss in a tactful and considerate manner.

Breaking off a Kiss

PULLING BACK Pulling back gently can be a good way to end a kiss, and Lisa tries to end this one by moving back slightly. Notice that the movement need only be subtle: she still has her hands on his shoulders, yet she *has* pulled back from the kiss.

RESTING FOREHEADS TOGETHER Another way to end a kiss is to rest your forehead against your partner, as Lisa does here. This enables her to pivot her mouth away from his, which is a clear signal that she wants to stop. At this point Lewis seems to take the hint and he stops kissing too.

RUBBING NOSES PLAYFULLY A gentle rub of the noses is a nice way to conclude a kissing session. It wordlessly says you had fun and it tells your partner that you're not stopping because you dislike him. Rubbing noses can be quite playful and romantic.

MAKING EYE CONTACT Looking Lewis in the eye is another way Lisa signals that there are no hard feelings even though the kissing has stopped. At this point he knows she's serious about breaking off the kiss, even though his puzzled expression suggests that he doesn't really understand *why* she stopped.

Kissing
on a
Park Bench

KISSING ON A BENCH is one of the all-time most fun things to do in a park, but few people realize the full romantic potential of this innocent pastime. One person who *does* know how to get the most out of the experience is Woody Allen, and there's a great park bench kissing scene in the concluding moments of *Annie Hall* (1977) between Alvy (Woody Allen) and Annie (Diane Keaton). All the key essentials of kissing on a park bench appear in this short scene.

Alvy begins the kiss with his arm around Annie, the two of them sitting with their backs against the bench in a relaxed position. The placement of his arm around her lends a cozy feeling to the kiss, and even though they're in public and can be seen by passersby, he's sheltering her from the world and at the same time calling attention to the fact that they're a couple. He's not doing this in an overly possessive way or distracting her from what's happening around them in the park; instead, he's enjoying their time together, his other arm resting casually on the back of the bench, suggesting that he's in a relaxed mood.

His follow-through after the kiss is also excellent as they laugh together and look at each other for a moment. After kissing on a park bench it's often nice to keep the good feelings going with some upbeat words or a joke. Sitting on a park bench might be a rather dull affair were it not for the fact that it's in a nice location and affords an ever-changing view of nature and of the people who pass by. In fact, people watching can stimulate your imagination and lead to other great kisses when the moment is right. Alvy notices something interesting occurring in front of them, so he points it out to Annie and they both turn their attention to it. In this way a simple kiss on a park bench has evolved into a pleasant interlude that goes beyond the kiss itself. Any park-bench kiss can be a fun experience if you remember to incorporate some of these key elements, turning the focus from the two of you out toward the park, and then back to yourselves in an ever-changing interaction.

Kissing on a
Park Bench

A PUBLIC KISS This kiss is done in public, for all the world to see, but at the same time the bench affords a little bit of privacy. As soon as you sit on a park bench it becomes in some sense yours, and you can enjoy a bit of cozy romance without being interrupted, as Alvy and Annie are doing here.

AFTER THE KISS Kissing on a park bench will usually produce a happy, relaxed feeling, as it seems to have done for Alvy and Annie.

MOVING OUT After focusing on themselves, Alvy lets his attention widen to include the immediate environment. Keeping his arm around Annie, he shares his observations with her.

PEOPLE WATCHING A park bench is an ideal spot for people watching, and once you see someone or something of interest you can talk about it—and then get back to kissing.

Kissing Someone Who's Crying

WHEN SOMEONE YOU LOVE cries, soft words and a hug might help, but kissing is a surefire way to make her feel a little better. Of course it depends on the reason she's crying, but if it has anything to do with you and your relationship, a kiss at this emotionally charged moment can make all the difference. A good example of the way to kiss a crying person occurs in *Chocolat* (2000).

The scene begins when Vianne (Juliette Binoche) and Roux (Johnny Depp) go out for a boat ride and she begins to cry. The first thing to notice about Vianne is that when she cries she's still making eye contact with Roux. Although she has one hand raised to her forehead, the fact that she continues to look at him suggests that there's a connection between *why* she's crying and his presence. She has kept her feelings bottled up, and her tears are a signal that she's not content with her life. It's important to notice these clues to the *reason* why someone is crying because if she maintains eye contact with you through her tears, it may be a sign that there's something you can do to help. In the next moment Roux kisses her, but the interesting thing to note is that as soon as he gets close it's Vianne who is the more aggressive participant. She begins an open-mouth kiss, almost greedily kissing Roux back, leaning up so that her kisses can connect more powerfully and forcefully, opening and moving her mouth in a passionate manner that suggests she was simply waiting, even if only unconsciously, for this moment to occur and for these kisses to set her free. The turning point in her life is this moment of vulnerability where she gives in to her feelings and kisses Roux.

Johnny Depp's character approaches the situation with the utmost care and consideration, reaching out to softly and tentatively cradle the back of her head while continuing to kiss her. Most important of all, he kisses her back with the same force and passion. When kissing a crying person it's worth being extra sensitive to how she receives the kiss: if with gusto, as in the case of Vianne, kissing back with the same enthusiasm is appropriate.

When someone is emotionally upset, a kiss can transform her feelings to tears of joy, and in this case Roux pulls back from the kiss for a moment to see whether Vianne is still crying or has recovered. He looks at her sweetly, as if trying to understand her state of mind. In a situation like this, breaking off a kiss to assess your partner's state of mind is appropriate because without that information you might be kissing when she's not ready for it to continue. Vianne is clearly on the way to a full recovery from her upset state of mind because she jumps back into the kiss. This all goes to show that when you kiss a crying person, you're usually doing her, and yourself, a favor by helping her move on to a better state of mind and a happier feeling.

Kissing Someone Who's Crying

COMFORTING WITH A KISS When Roux comforts her with a kiss, Vianne gives as good as she gets, kissing him back with a surprising amount of passion and initiative, opening and closing her mouth, moving her head up, and basically confirming that he made the right decision to kiss her even though she was crying.

TENDER KISSING Although Vianne is kissing passionately, Roux seems to realize that a crying person needs a tender touch, so he extends his hand to cradle the back of her head. He also continues to kiss with tender kisses after her initial passion has subsided slightly.

JUDGING HER REACTION No one can read another person's mind, and it's a smart idea to do what Roux does—he breaks off for a moment to see how she's taking the kiss.

CONTINUING THE KISS A crying spell can be broken with a kiss, but sometimes it takes a series of kisses to cheer up your partner.

Quick Pecks

NOT ALL KISSES need be long drawn-out affairs. Some of the most memorable kisses are those quick little pecks you give to surprise or delight your partner. Such kisses are like appetizers, teasing and whetting the appetite in preparation for more sustained and substantial kisses to come. A very witty example of the quick peck and its proper execution appears in *Chaplin* (1992).

The sequence involving the peck opens with Chaplin (Robert Downey Jr.) walking along the set of one of his movies and spying Lita Grey (Deborah Moore), a silent-film star, being instructed by a cameraman. When the technician moves away, Chaplin moves in and leans down toward the young woman from behind. She's totally unaware of him and he moves very quickly, his lips closing in on her shoulder. The technique of executing a quick little peck in a surprise manner like this requires two things: nimbleness of movement and a certain playfulness of spirit. Nimbleness is especially necessary when giving a surprise peck because the recipient might move before your lips land. And a playful spirit is certainly helpful in executing a series of quick pecks because your partner is liable to break up laughing, as this silent-film star does when Chaplin kisses her.

Despite its brevity, the quick peck is not a kiss that can be relegated to the realm of mere kissing curiosities; indeed, the brevity of the kiss is out of all proportion to its effect. A quick peck executed in a fraction of a second can have more impact than a kiss that's long and drawn out—precisely because it's quick and punchy. Yet surprise alone can't account for the effectiveness of the quick peck in making recipients laugh. The feel of the lips hitting their mark in that instantaneous manner, the smacking sound, and the sudden withdrawal of the lips—all these things leave the recipient feeling a little breathless, as if someone had opened a conversation and then turned and walked away and smiled back coyly, batting the eyelashes in a flirtatious manner. The quick peck is the epitome of the flirtatious kiss. As used by Chaplin in this scene, it has its intended effect: Not only does it surprise Lita, but it tickles her fancy and brings a wonderful smile to her face. A series of quick pecks can be equally effective, if not more so, in delighting a partner who has grown bored with all your French kisses and long kisses. A quick peck is an excellent way to say hello and should never be underestimated. The quick peck Chaplin gives the silent-film star opens the door to a wonderful working relationship with her on the set, and your quick pecks may very well lead to equally satisfactory results.

Quick Pecks

OPPORTUNITY KNOCKS When Chaplin sees this lovely silent-film star waiting on the set, he gets the idea to move in for a quick peck on one of her bare shoulders. Notice that he prepares by taking off his cap, which might otherwise fall off or bump into her before the kiss.

MOVING IN FOR A KISS It takes a certain amount of speed and physical ability to execute a quick peck without giving yourself away. But a surprise kiss like this is almost always well received.

HITTING YOUR MARK The spot you kiss is just as important as the technique you use. Chaplin goes for the shoulder because it's almost inviting him with its prominence. The best spots for quick pecks are shoulders, arms, cheeks, or the back of the neck, provided hair isn't in the way.

GETTING A REACTION This reaction is just what Chaplin had hoped for. A quick peck can boost a person's spirit and lead to a happy feeling that can persist for hours. In this case, the two went on to work together on a number of successful scenes, probably due in large part to the way Chaplin introduced himself to her with a quick peck.

Kissing While Dancing

KISSING WHILE DANCING is a wonderful way to get even closer than dancing alone allows, and it's also a form of public kissing that tells the world the two of you are a couple. A good example of the technique appears in *Circle of Friends* (1995) between Jack (Chris O'Donnell) and Bernadette (Minnie Driver). The kiss occurs on a crowded dance floor, which makes it a tricky procedure, but these two carry it off with aplomb.

Of course it's easier to kiss when slow dancing, as Jack and Bernadette are in this scene. When dancing like this, proper form requires the man and the woman to place their heads to the side of their partner's so that each one is, in effect, looking over the other's shoulder. This makes it easy to simply move the heads back and touch lips. In the excitement of the moment they have also temporarily closed their eyes, as most people do when kissing. To close your eyes on a dance floor, however, is a more dangerous proposition than to close them in a parlor on a love seat, but when done for just a moment during a slow dance, as in this scene, it shouldn't pose much risk.

Both Jack and Bernadette then lean slightly back, their eyes still closed as they break off the kiss. This allows them to interact and whisper a few endearments, rub noses, and cuddle affectionately. Jack and Bernadette are contentedly smiling at each other, wordlessly saying that they're in love. Notice that their heads are still facing forward, allowing for maximum interaction and the possibility of conversation and direct eye contact. In the next moment, they move their heads into the more standard dancing position at the side of their partner. Bernadette is smiling with pleasure at this point, and very quickly and impulsively, as she moves her head to Jack's side, she does something that's unusual for a dancing kiss but that's also a technically brilliant move: She nuzzles her nose into Jack's cheek, showing him that she really cares and is enjoying the experience of kissing and dancing with him. This little teasing motion marks her as a sophisticated kisser, one who brings a sense of playfulness and flirtation to the kiss.

Kissing while dancing is certainly not for the shy, as these two are surrounded by scores of onlookers. Although not every couple will be the center of attraction on a dance floor, for some this is precisely what gives the whole experience its special charm.

Kissing While Dancing

KISSING ON A DANCE FLOOR Kissing on a dance floor can be a big moment for a couple. Here Jack and Bernadette show the crowd that they're not afraid to be seen kissing each other. The longer such a kiss lasts, the further you'll move across the dance floor and the more people will see you smooching.

FACE TO FACE From this position Jack and Bernadette can gaze lovingly into each other's eyes or simply rest their foreheads together like lovebirds. Coming out of a kiss to find themselves surrounded by people, they probably want to stay in their own private world awhile longer.

BREAKING INTO A GRIN When Bernadette realizes what she just did, she breaks into a grin of pleasure.

NUZZLING HER PARTNER Bernadette nuzzles her nose into Jack's cheek—a fitting conclusion to their first kiss while dancing.

Kissing at Sea

KISSING AT SEA has its special rewards—you're out in the open air, the scenery can be breathtakingly beautiful, and the movement of the ocean itself can impart a pleasant rhythm to the experience. Everyone should try kissing at sea at least once, if only to discover a new place and location for a romantic encounter. One of the most memorable kisses at sea occurs at the end of *Dr. No* (1962) between James Bond (Sean Connery) and Honey (Ursula Andress). Their kiss occurs in a small boat on the open sea.

In this scene Bond and Honey have just escaped from the island of Doctor No and are in a motorboat that's being towed back to safety by some friendly Americans. The relationship between Bond and Honey has been moving closer and closer ever since they met days ago, and they're now in each other's arms. As their launch is towed along behind the American ship, Bond and Honey kiss, enjoying the ride they're getting from their new friends, relishing the fresh air, and basking in the warm sunshine.

Their work is completed, Bond's mission is a success, and they're finally going home. As would be expected in such a situation, they haven't a care in the world, and they act like two people in love, embracing and kissing as the waves rock their small craft back and forth.

But kissing at sea exposes anyone who tries it to the challenge of dealing with those waves, which here are rocking the boat so much that anyone but a James Bond might get seasick. In fact, Bond and Honey manage to keep their mouths together despite the high speed of the towship and the jostling of their little launch. They surely know that within a short time they'll be surrounded by people who want to wish them well and who will certainly congratulate them on a successful mission, but they want their privacy now. At this point, Bond loosens the tow line and, without breaking off his kiss, lets it slip off the launch and into the water. As this is happening, Honey looks on with some amusement, without even breaking off the kiss herself. Finally, their little motorboat is untethered, their friends are speeding off ahead, and Honey and Bond are free to kiss to their hearts' content.

The key to fully enjoying romantic kisses at sea is to let go of the rest of the world and enjoy your special romantic hideaway on the high seas.

Kissing at Sea

GOING HOME The conclusion of *Dr. No* finds the hero going home in a launch towed by his friends from the U.S. Coast Guard. All's well that ends well, but Bond still has some surprises in store for the viewer.

BRAVING THE ELEMENTS Kissing on the open sea is not for people who easily get seasick but is great for those who like action and adventure, who enjoy nature at its best, and who like the smell of fresh air and the feel of rocking waves.

KISSING AT SEA Bond's first romantic kiss with his companion, Honey, occurs in a motorboat in the final seconds of the film. The kiss is romantic because they're alone in that little launch together.

LETTING THE WORLD GO Their kiss is also funny because Bond lets the tow line go. The message from this scene is clear: Find your own special place to be alone when you kiss at sea— or anywhere else, for that matter.

Kissing Against a Wall

SOMETIMES IT'S NICE to lean against a wall while kissing. The technique is illustrated in *Crazy/Beautiful* (2001) when Carlos (Jay Hernandez) kisses Nicole (Kirsten Dunst). Before you kiss against a wall, though, it's a good idea to establish a playful mood. These two are a new couple, enjoying each other's company, and by the time they get to *this* kiss they've already been dating for a while and are ready to enjoy a new experience.

Nicole rests her back against the wall and puts her hands on the boy's shoulders. Carlos stands in front of her, about a foot away, his hands placed gently on her hips. This basic position has a number of advantages, not the least of which is that it allows the girl to relax while being kissed. Nicole and Carlos are doing the kiss at school in front of numerous passersby who don't even stop to gawk, and this underscores the casual nature of the technique and the way that it fits seamlessly into a modern urban environment. It really won't attract much attention, especially if done in an informal and relaxed way, as this one is. When Carlos breaks off momentarily, Nicole raises her hands from his shoulders, intending to adjust her position and get more comfortable. Carlos senses that she's enjoying herself and he's happy to see that she's comfortable and relaxed. Nicole adjusts the position of her hands and arms, putting her elbows and forearms on his neck, and Carlos smiles, apparently aware that she's settling in for an extended kiss against the wall. Back into the kiss they go, both of them content and at ease, paying no attention to their classmates who are walking nearby. Kissing against a wall like this is a pleasant change from the more formal heart-to-heart kiss, in which lovers hug each other. In this case, they have the wall behind Nicole as a prop, and they make full use of it to relax into the kiss. Perhaps they're even showing off a little since they're kissing in public.

BACK AGAINST THE WALL Nicole and Carlos are kissing with her back resting comfortably against the brick wall while her boyfriend stands in front of her.

HEAD AGAINST THE WALL Notice that Nicole also has her head resting against the wall. Although this position prevents her from leaning back to adjust the pressure of the kiss, she can still move her head from side to side.

CHANGING POSITIONS Nicole is changing the position of her arms. As a kiss against a wall deepens, the person against the wall may wish to relax even more, and placing the arms higher up on your partner's shoulders can make you feel more comfortable.

ARMS ON SHOULDERS It's easy to see why kissing against a wall is so popular. Nicole and Carlos are having a great time, and it's the easiest kiss in the world to do: all you need are two willing kissers—and a wall.

Kissing Across a Table

THE IDEA OF kissing across a table has undoubtedly occurred to many couples in restaurants, and not a few have actually tried the technique. This may be because the kiss offers rewards on so many levels: It's romantic, it says you're a couple, it's a public kiss, and it's a wonderful little appetizer for the meal. A perfect example of how it can be accomplished with ease appears in *The Good Girl* (2002). The kiss between Justine (Jennifer Aniston) and Holden (Jake Gyllenhaal) happens at a picnic-style table outside an informal restaurant during a date.

The setting itself is conducive to this kiss because there are no crowds of onlookers to distract them. Kissing across a table is a rather informal procedure which might be trickier inside a five-star restaurant with a wider table, yet even there it could be done when the moment is right and no one is focusing attention on the couple. At the start of the scene, Justine and Holden are enjoying a conversation and seem comfortable with each other's company. It naturally helps to make sure your partner is in the right frame of mind before you kiss across a table because the move can be a surprise and might cause the recipient to sit back in astonishment. Justine ensures that Holden is ready for the kiss by looking at him carefully while talking. He smiles and even leans forward, and she knows that now the moment is right: not only is he in an upbeat frame of mind, but he has leaned slightly across the table himself, setting up the possibility of a kiss.

The technical requirements of the kiss are minimal, but they do involve some degree of physical dexterity since the kisser must rise into a squatting position over her seat and lean forward. In some cases where the table is narrow enough, you needn't rise at all, all you have to do is lean across the table and kiss. But in this setting, since the table is rather wide, Justine needs to rise into a squatting position and then bend slightly toward Holden. This is exactly what she does, kissing the rather surprised Holden full on the lips. The kiss itself lasts only a second or two, and then she sits back down and smiles at him. Kissing across a table like this is a show-offy move that's definitely worth a try when you're in the mood for romantic fun.

Kissing Across a Table

THE OBSTACLE IS THE TABLE Lovers face many obstacles, but here the primary obstacle is an inanimate object, the table itself, which lies between them.

SHE WATCHES HIM Justine is looking at Holden to see whether he might be ready for a kiss. More than this, she's trying to judge whether she can reach him if she leans across the table.

HE LOOKS READY Holden makes it easy for her by looking ready to receive a kiss. Sometimes you must wait for the right moment before kissing across a table.

SHE RISES FOR THE KISS Notice that Holden doesn't rise for the kiss, the entire burden is on Justine because she's the one who initiated it. It's certainly worth the effort. There's always a small thrill from doing this one, especially when others can see you.

Kissing in Water

KISSING IN THE OCEAN or in a pool almost always subtly changes a kissing experience, making it more playful and fun. An excellent example of how to kiss in water appears in *Cake* (2005) when Pippa (Heather Graham) kisses Ian (David Sutcliffe) on a beautiful hazy afternoon in Georgian Bay, adjacent to Lake Huron in Canada.

The scene begins when Pippa finds Ian in the bay, runs up to him, and the two frolic playfully. Their horseplay involves both of them slightly losing their balance and almost dancing around in the water. Once Pippa gets things going, she moves to the next step and jokingly kisses Ian. He replies with enthusiasm and joins in the fun. The kiss already has a light and airy feel because it's occurring in water, and they keep it this way throughout. One of the nicest touches that Pippa adds occurs when she stops during the kiss and places her hands on Ian's shoulders and smiles up at him, wordlessly saying she loves him. When surrounded by water, it's a good idea to take a break like this now and then to get your bearings—or your balance—and be romantic.

The experience of kissing in water varies depending on how deep the two kissers are. In this scene, they're only knee deep, but still the water has added a lighthearted feeling to everything, especially their kiss. Even when they break off to gaze at each other, it doesn't have the serious and heavy connotations it might have if done on land. It's actually a very romantic moment, and after it's over they get right back to kissing, this time with Pippa locking her hands behind Ian's neck. Ian stands steady and gazes back at her. Pippa uses great technique here, holding Ian and surrendering to the feeling of the kiss by resting her weight against him. For his part, Ian is totally into the moment, which is the way it usually is when immersed in water like this, and he returns her kisses very tenderly.

After the kiss the two hug for a while, with Pippa placing her hands flat on Ian's back and tightly clasping him to her chest, resting her chin on his shoulder and closing her eyes. By her expression alone we get a feel for the intensity of the kiss and what it means to her. We also see that she's creating her own special world, surrounded by water and holding Ian tightly. The bottom line is that a kiss in water can add a charming amount of spontaneity, playfulness, and fun to the experience, and for this reason it's highly recommended when you find yourself in the right watery environment.

Kissing in Water

TESTING THE WATERS Pippa tests the waters with a few experimental kisses while Ian stands knee-deep in the bay. Once they see how much fun this can be, they enjoy a few more kisses in the water.

TAKING A BREAK Here they take a short break to laugh and gaze at each other. It's evident from Ian's expression that he liked being surprised with a kiss while he was in the water.

SHARING THE FUN Water has a way of uniting lovers, surrounding and linking them in a manner that can't easily be duplicated on land. Because of the watery location, Pippa and Ian find themselves united in an especially sweet and tender embrace.

OVER-THE-SHOULDER HUG Taking another break, they hug momentarily, still surrounded by the water and still linked in a way that land-locked kisses would have a hard time mimicking.

Kissing While Laughing

ALMOST EVERYONE LAUGHS or giggles on occasion while kissing, but some people take it as a personal insult and a comment on their *own* kissing style when their partner does this. But in most cases they're not laughing *at* you, they're simply laughing because it feels good. A perfect example of how laughing or giggling can fit nicely into a kissing session (without insulting the kissing partner) appears in *Stay Hungry* (1976). The kiss between Joe (Arnold Schwarzenegger) and Mary (Sally Field) occurs in a bodybuilding gym.

Schwarzenegger is playing the role of a bodybuilder competing for the Mr. Universe title. Sally Field is a gymnast who's one of his good friends. The scene opens as Mary comes into the gym, spots Joe, and runs up to him in glee, jumping into his arms. The hulking Joe easily catches her and holds her as she looks at him and says how happy she is to see him again. Then she kisses him a few times, a series of quick little friendly kisses on the cheek. During these initial kisses, Joe remains rather serious. He continues to hold Mary in his arms and doesn't kiss back or even open his mouth to say anything.

But Mary is just bubbling over with happiness and she pauses to look at him to see how serious he is. Unable to contain her joy at seeing him again, she begins a second series of quick little kisses, this time nuzzling her nose into Joe's cheek and face. This is the move that Joe can't resist. He smiles involuntarily at her and then begins to giggle. When he giggles, Mary continues kissing him. The fact that Joe is laughing doesn't stop her for a second, and this is the best way to deal with a laughing partner: keep on kissing. In fact, once he starts laughing she kisses him even more fervently, as if she knows that he's just giggling because he's glad to see her.

Joe even kisses Mary back a few times while he's still giggling and laughing. For the person who giggles during a kiss, this too is the best way to deal with it: simply continue kissing even when you find yourself laughing. Your happiness will be communicated through your giggles and kisses to your partner. In other words, like Joe, keep kissing and don't worry that you're insulting your partner. If she has any sense, like Mary does, she'll realize that you're enjoying yourself—not criticizing her.

Finally, Joe hugs Mary, happy to see her again. Laughing while kissing has helped Joe and Mary say hello, and it can work the same way for you if you simply let the laughs happen.

Kissing While Laughing

STAYING SERIOUS Joe stays serious at the outset of their encounter, but his attitude doesn't stop Mary from giving him a series of greeting kisses on the cheek.

LAUGHING Finally, Joe can't resist any longer and he begins to giggle. Notice that Mary has stopped to look at him, but she says nothing about the fact that he's laughing. In most cases laughter needs no comment and you can go on kissing without saying a word.

KISSING WHILE LAUGHING Joe is kissing while giggling. You can see that his eyes are crinkled up in laughter. Because laughter is so contagious, if one person laughs the other may start laughing too, and in this scene that's exactly what happens. You can see Mary giggling as she kisses him.

SHARING THE JOY When people realize that laughter means that someone is having fun, they can get on with their kissing and hugging—as Joe and Mary do. A wise kisser knows that laughing while kissing means enjoyment.

Repeated Kissing

SOMETIMES—in fact *most* of the time—a single kiss just isn't enough. This is where repeated kissing comes into play. A wonderfully comic version of repeated kissing appears in *Spanglish* (2004) when John (Adam Sandler) is kissed by his wife, Deborah (Téa Leoni), one afternoon in their bedroom. Her kiss is meant to congratulate him on receiving a good newspaper review.

The technique of repeated kissing begins, of course, with the first in the series of kisses. Usually this kind of kissing starts slowly and softly and then gradually builds in intensity. However, since this is a comedy, things are exaggerated and Deborah actually starts quite intensely, with very complete coverage of John's mouth with her own, wrapping one hand behind his head, and passionately open-mouth kissing him. Adam Sandler's comic genius is everywhere present in this scene as we hear his character interject remarks about Deborah's technique while she's kissing him.

After the initial kiss Deborah leans back for a moment, catch–

ing her breath, surveying the territory of John's mouth for a renewed attack. When she leans in for the second kiss, she nearly knocks the breath out of him, and the stunned husband cannot speak—his lips are pursed, his jaw and face are crinkled, and his head is rocked back as Deborah kisses him even more passionately than before. Of course in real life repeated kissing isn't always this dramatic and energetic, yet the basic concept of increasing the intensity of the kisses is perfectly valid.

It should be pointed out that the technique of repeated kissing usually involves kisses that are nearly identical—that is, *all* lip kisses, for example, rather than a lip kiss followed by a cheek kiss followed by a neck kiss. The key to this technique lies in the pacing and tempo of the kisses, which should build to a climax, as they do here. After the second kiss, Deborah breaks off yet again, and this time when she opens her mouth she looks like a shark, hungry and aggressive, leaning in for a monumental kiss which connects with such passion and power that we're surprised John is left standing after it's over.

Kisses that increase in passion and power are the secret to repeated kissing, and if you use this technique with even half the vigor present in this scene from *Spanglish,* you're sure to have a very impressed recipient.

Repeated Kissing

TAKING AIM Pulling back for a moment, Deborah paces herself carefully and prepares for the next kiss. The look of concentration on her face says it all: Think before you kiss. By thinking about what you're going to do next, your repeated kisses will have more precision and passion.

HITTING THE MARK In this brilliant comic exaggeration, John looks like he's been hit by a truck. The comedy, however, doesn't diminish the message—repeated kissing is a good technique and can be used to good effect, especially when you increase the intensity of each kiss, as Deborah is doing here.

OPEN-MOUTH KISSING For the next in the series, Deborah is clearly increasing the intensity, opening her mouth wide and using her hand behind John's head to close the gap with force. This is a laugh-out-loud scene.

REPEATED PERFORMANCE The final kiss nearly stuns John senseless. Clearly, Deborah has increased the intensity! Repeated kissing (with a little less force) can actually be quite romantic, suggesting that the kisser is passionate and full of strong desire.

How to Stop an Argument with a Kiss

QUITE OFTEN even bitter arguments can be completely turned around and transformed into the sweetest of kisses. A perfect example of how to stop an argument with a kiss occurs in *Love Story* (1970) when Jennifer (Ali MacGraw) kisses Oliver (Ryan O'Neal) in Harvard Yard on a snowy afternoon.

The prerequisite to stopping an argument with a kiss is that the two participants be in love, or on the verge of falling in love, because if love is the real basis of their relationship, a kiss can bring that positive feeling back to the surface. Oliver, who comes from a wealthy family and stands to inherit millions, is falling in love with Jennifer, who comes from humbler roots and is also falling in love with him. In this scene they're arguing primarily out of frustration and a need to feel understood. These are elements common to all relationships, and the conflict between Jennifer and Oliver is one that every person who has been in love can understand. She wants him to empathize with her, he wants her to understand him, and they're both afraid that their partner will reject them and consider them foolish. As they walk along, their argument escalates until it can only end in one of two ways: They can separate or they can reconcile. In this case a happy outcome occurs when they pause and look into each other's eyes and suddenly realize that they've been arguing because they want to be closer together, not further apart.

The kiss commences when they stop talking and turn to each other to find the truth about what their relationship really is. Looking into Jennifer's eyes, Ryan is astonished to discover that she's looking back with an open expression and the hint of a smile. Looking at Oliver, Jennifer is surprised to see that he's not really angry with her after all, he's simply frustrated and feeling alone. At that moment, when they look at each other with open hearts and open minds, they're poised for one of the most romantic kisses possible, a kiss that stops an argument and transforms it into a wonderful connection. Even as they close the gap between them in preparation for the kiss, they're both smiling because this is what they've really wanted all along.

The kiss that stops an argument, like this one, needn't be protracted or overly sexual. The connection and the couple's true feelings are the important elements, and in this case Oliver presses his mouth forcibly to Jennifer's and raises his hands to caress her face, in effect saying that he has love in his heart and is glad they're not arguing. Jennifer kisses back with a sweet and gentle acknowledgment that she had not really wanted to argue either. Kissing like this can do more than stop an argument; ultimately it can also let love unite two people whose hearts are in the same place and who realize that they would rather be kissing than fighting.

How to Stop an Argument with a Kiss

UNWILLING TO COMPROMISE Jennifer at first *seems* unwilling to compromise, and many arguments stem from a misperception like this. But as subsequent actions will show, she's not as inflexible as she appears.

FEELING MISUNDERSTOOD Oliver feels misunderstood, which is why he's raising his voice. Most arguments involve one or both participants feeling misunderstood. Once this issue is resolved, he'll start to feel better about being with Jennifer.

MOVING TOGETHER Jennifer and Oliver move together in order to resolve their differences with a kiss. They've stopped arguing and both are smiling in anticipation of the kiss, hoping that their reconciliation will last.

KISSING AWAY MISUNDERSTANDING The kiss symbolizes a reconciliation and helps smooth over their differences. It says that they have better things to do than argue. The pleasure they receive from the kiss also helps calm their spirits and makes them feel loved.

Slow Kissing

ONE ADVANCED KISSING TECHNIQUE that's too often overlooked is slow kissing. A brilliant example of slow kissing occurs in Steve Buscemi's *Trees Lounge* (1996). Debbie (Chloe Sevigny) and Tommy (Steve Buscemi) are on the floor after engaging in some flirtatious wrestling. What you do *before* a slow kiss is sometimes just as important as the kiss itself because if you do something fun and romantic it can come back into your mind during the kiss, providing you with beautiful mental pictures and emotions that will fuel the action. Tommy begins by leaning over Debbie and looking at her mouth. He's taking his time and so should you.

Tommy leans over Debbie and lets his lips hang less than an inch above her mouth, poised, ready, and waiting. This waiting serves an important purpose by preparing your partner for the kiss and heightening the romantic tension between you. The pause almost forces your minds to work at anticipating what will happen next, and anticipation can sometimes be half the fun.

Once his lips do connect, Tommy takes his time with the kiss. Debbie is in no hurry either, and the two of them are now on the same wavelength. Both Debbie and Tommy deliberately break off the kiss now and then to enjoy the moment. Stopping occasionally is one of the most important ways to slow a kiss. You simply pull back slightly and pause for a few seconds. Another essential technique for slowing a kiss is illustrated when Tommy puts his head beside Debbie's and kisses her cheek and ear. The smile on Debbie's face says it all. Remember to slow down your next kissing session and you'll put a similar smile on your partner's face.

Slow Kissing

LIKE DREAMING If you flirt before a kiss and have fun, images and emotions can come back during the kiss itself so that you'll feel like you're dreaming. Such mental activity slows down your kisses so you get more from them.

SLOW MOTION Imagine that you're under water in order to slow down your kisses. This trick is especially useful in delaying an approach. Notice that Tommy is taking his time, looking at Debbie before he makes lip contact.

PAUSING FOR EFFECT Slow your kissing down by breaking off and hovering over your partner like Tommy is doing here. You can learn to slow your kisses by slowing how fast you eat. Most Westerners eat—and kiss—too fast.

BREAKING OFF MOMENTARILY Take a break now and then from lip kisses and let your lips stray to her cheek and ear. Such breaks are like resting and will enable you to come back to her lips with more passion.

APPENDIX ONE

Film Title List (Alphabetical)

The Cooler (2003) 120

Crazy/Beautiful (2001) 191

Cruel Intentions (1999) 123

Cry-Baby (1990) 78

Dirty Dancing (1987) 90

La Dolce vita (1960) 164

Dr. No (1962) 188

Eyes Wide Shut (1999) 149

Ghost (1990) 99

Gone With the Wind (1939) 96

The Good Girl (2002) 194

The House of the Spirits (1993) 135

Jane Eyre (1996) 57

The Locusts (1997) 51

Love Story (1970) 206

Loves of a Blonde (1965) 161

The Majestic (2001) 66

The Man Who Cried (2000) 54

Meet Joe Black (1998) 75

Mostly Martha (2001) 102

Mulholland Drive (2001) 138

The Notebook (2004) 129

Notting Hill (1999) 155

An Officer and a Gentleman (1982) 9

The Philadelphia Story (1940) 18

The Piano (1993) 12

Pleasantville (1998) 132

Pretty Woman (1990) 42

The Prince of Tides (1991) 142

Proof (2005) 60

Raging Bull (1980) 36

Sabrina (1954) 84

She's the One (1996) 24

Spanglish (2004) 203

Stay Hungry (1976) 200

A Streetcar Named Desire (1951) 27

The Thomas Crown Affair (1968) 39
Titanic (1997) 170
To Die For (1995) 21
To Have and Have Not (1944) 111
Top Gun (1986) 105
Trees Lounge (1996) 209
Two Girls and a Guy (1997) 81
When Harry Met Sally (1989) 69
Wide Sargasso Sea (1993) 87
William Shakespeare's Romeo + Juliet (1996) 146
You've Got Mail (1998) 45

APPENDIX TWO

Film Title List (Chronological)

Gone With the Wind (1939) 96
The Philadelphia Story (1940) 18
Casablanca (1942) 3
To Have and Have Not (1944) 111
A Streetcar Named Desire (1951) 27
Sabrina (1954) 84
Bus Stop (1956) 15
An Affair to Remember (1957) 114
La Dolce vita (1960) 164
Dr. No (1962) 188
Loves of a Blonde (1965) 161
The Thomas Crown Affair (1968) 39
Love Story (1970) 206
Stay Hungry (1976) 200
Annie Hall (1977) 176
Raging Bull (1980) 36
An Officer and a Gentleman (1982) 9
Top Gun (1986) 105
Dirty Dancing (1987) 90
Bull Durham (1988) 48

When Harry Met Sally (1989) 69
Cry-Baby (1990) 78
Ghost (1990) 99
Pretty Woman (1990) 42
The Prince of Tides (1991) 142
Chaplin (1992) 182
Coneheads (1993) 126
The House of the Spirits (1993) 135
The Piano (1993) 12
Wide Sargasso Sea (1993) 87
Circle of Friends (1995) 185
To Die For (1995) 21
Bed of Roses (1996) 173
Jane Eyre (1996) 57
She's the One (1996) 24
Trees Lounge (1996) 209
William Shakespeare's Romeo + Juliet (1996) 146
Breaking Up (1997) 30
The Locusts (1997) 51
Titanic (1997) 170
Two Girls and a Guy (1997) 81
City of Angels (1998) 108
Meet Joe Black (1998) 75
Pleasantville (1998) 132
You've Got Mail (1998) 45
Cruel Intentions (1999) 123
Eyes Wide Shut (1999) 149
Notting Hill (1999) 155
Bounce (2000) 167
Chocolat (2000) 179
The Man Who Cried (2000) 54
A Beautiful Mind (2001) 6
Bridget Jones's Diary (2001) 63
Crazy/Beautiful (2001) 191
The Majestic (2001) 66
Mostly Martha (2001) 102

APPENDIX THREE

Actor List (Alphabetical)

Index

Photo Credits

Photo Credits

ABOUT THE AUTHOR

Author of the international bestseller *The Art of Kissing,* William Cane is the pen name of Michael Christian. Educated at Fordham College, Boston College, Boston College Law School, and Boston University, he practiced law briefly in 1986 before switching careers. He taught English at Boston College for fourteen years and today is a frequent lecturer at colleges and universities across the country. In 2001 he produced the documentary version of *The Art of Kissing* and in 2004 he wrote the off-off-Broadway musical *Meet the Real Ernest Shackleton.* He lives in Jersey City, New Jersey, with his wife.

Sometimes you need to Kiss *and* Tell!

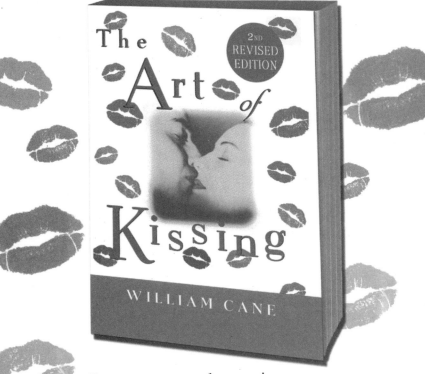

2ND REVISED EDITION

The Art of Kissing

WILLIAM CANE

Prepare to pucker-up! With colorful examples, fun facts, techniques and tips, plus fascinating survey results, the second revised edition reveals what men and women like most—*and least*—about kissing, and lessons on how to give your special someone what they want. It includes seven new kisses, more on the all-important French kiss, plus a few more expert secrets to smooching!

Available Wherever Books Are Sold

St. Martin's Griffin   www.kissing.com